AIMING FOR EXCELLENCE

YARRA
THEOLOGICAL
UNION
1972-2022

EDITED BY
PETER MALONE

COVENTRY PRESS

Published in Australia by
Coventry Press
33 Scoresby Road
Bayswater VIC 3153

ISBN 9781922589248

Compilation Copyright © Christopher Monaghan CP 2022
Copyright of individual articles remains with the contributors

All rights reserved. Other than for the purposes and subject to the conditions prescribed under the *Copyright Act*, no part of this publication may be reproduced, stored in a retrieval system, or transmitted in any form or by any means, electronic, mechanical, photocopying, recording or otherwise, without the prior permission of the publisher.

Catalogue-in-Publication entry is available from the National Library of Australia http://catalogue.nla.gov.au

Cover design by Ian James – www.jgd.com.au
Text design by Coventry Press
Set in Fontin

Printed in Australia

Table of Contents

Foreword
    Peter Sherlock   7

The Origins and Beginnings of the
Yarra Theological Union
    Peter Malone MSC   10

Fifty Memories   21

    Michael Kelly   22
    Paul Chandler   26
    Tony Kelly   30
    Tom McDonough   33
    John Mulrooney   36
    Rose Marie Prosser   38
    Paul Beirne   41
    Anneliese Reinhard   44
    Mary Scarfe   47
    Maryanne Confoy   51
    Stephen Hackett   54
    Sue Phillips   59
    Ann Lorkin   63
    Bernadette Micallef   66
    Bruce Duncan   70
    Stephen Bliss   75
    Aloysius Rego   79
    Mary Coloe   83
    Anne Hunt   87

Vincent Long	90
Tim Norton	92
Michael Hardie	96
Mary Reaburn	99
Mark O'Brien	103
Chris Chaplin	107
Kathleen Williams	111
Robyn Reynolds	115
Matthew Beckman	117
Rosie Joyce	120
John N. Collins	122
Cecilia Francisco-Tan	125
Catherine McCahill	130
Claire Renkin	133
Ross Fishburn	136
John C. McDowel	139
Peter Whiting	143
Gavin Brown	146
Ben Ho	149
Jonathan Rowe	153
Brian Gallagher	156
Philip Malone	159
Eva Dabasy	163
Margaret Smith	167
Margaret Bentley	172
Carmel Posa	175
Pia Pagotto	179
Susan Richardson	182
Gary Harkin	186
Daniel Magadia	188
Janette Elliott	193

The School of Indigenous Studies at
the University of Divinity   199

National Centre for Pastoral research   202

Postscript   203
    The YTU Yacht: Revue 1983
        Tony Kelly CSsR   203

Looking Forward to What Comes Next in our Life
        Christopher Monaghan CP   207

Memories (in alphabetical order)

    Matthew Beckman
    Paul Beirne
    Margaret Bentley
    Stephen Bliss
    Gavin Brown
    Paul Chandler
    Chris Chaplin
    John Collins
    Mary Coloe
    Maryanne Confoy
    Eva Dabasy
    Bruce Duncan
    Janette Elliott
    Ross Fishburn
    Cecilia Francisco-Tan
    Brian Gallagher
    Stephen Hackett
    Michael Hardie
    Gary Harkin
    Ben Ho

Anne Hunt
Rosie Joyce
Michael Kelly
Tony Kelly
Vincent Long
Ann Lorkin
Daniel Magadia
Philip Malone
Rose Marie Prosser
Catherine McCahill
Tom McDonough
John McDowell
Bernadette Micallef
John Mulrooney
Tim Norton
Mark O'Brien
Pia Pagotto
Sue Phillips
Carmel Posa
Mary Reaburn
Aloysius Rego
Anneliese Reinhard
Claire Renkin
Robyn Reynolds
Sue Richardson
Jonathan Rowe
Mary Scarfe
Margaret Smith
Peter Whiting
Kathleen Williams

Foreword

PETER SHERLOCK, VICE-CHANCELLOR, UNIVERSITY OF DIVINITY

In Leviticus 25, the people of God are instructed to celebrate a jubilee every fifty years. The concept is modelled on God's order for creation, the sabbath rest on the seventh day. For the fiftieth year is the sabbath of sabbaths, following seven sabbatical cycles of seven years.

A jubilee is a holy year. It is a time for sounding the trumpet (not just any trumpet, but the LOUD trumpet) throughout all the land. It is a time for forgiveness, rest and renewal.

European Christians have adapted the ancient Hebrew celebration of the Jubilee in myriad ways, from the Holy Years proclaimed by the Pope to the royal jubilees celebrated by Christian monarchs. In the academy, it became the sabbatical, the practice of faculty taking one year in every seven as a year of rest from teaching to make room for an intense period of research and writing – though outside of YTU, few if any academics make it to their seventh sabbatical.

2022 is Yarra Theological Union's first Jubilee Year. Founded in 1972, YTU (along with its sister institution Catholic Theological College) took up the spirit of Vatican II, as an innovative collaboration of religious congregations participating in tertiary education within the even wider ecumenical environment of what is now the University of Divinity. Indeed, 2022 is a Jubilee Year for the University too as the fiftieth anniversary of the Roman Catholic Church becoming one of its sponsors and members in what remains an early, exceptional and enduring expression of our heartfelt search for unity in Christ.

A Jubilee Year is a time for forgiveness, for rest and renewal. It is fitting then that this collection of reflections from YTU staff, students and graduates constitutes a rich and rewarding testament to the College's distinctive ethos, drawn from its many spiritual traditions.

At its heart, YTU is focused on the mission of gospel service, the sharing of the good news and of its implications for justice and equity in the world. This is expressed by YTU's warm embrace of staff and students through its hospitality and deep pastoral spirit, where everyone is counted dear and where no-one is left behind. Then there is the amazing YTU ability to adapt – to 'make do' – with whatever resources its members can muster, leavened by a strong sense of humour.

I hope that you, like me, may read this collection as a means of rest and renewal, one which allows you to call forth your experience of YTU. My experiences include the creative peace and beauty of the St Paschal's estate (where it is a joy for me and my staff to be YTU's new neighbour). There is the incredible passion and commitment of staff, the brilliant teachers who draw on wisdom born of deep experience and exceptional scholarship for their students, and the diverse student body preparing for challenges both known and unknown, here in Australia and around the world. There is the food and wine, fellowship and music, which restores and renews our humanity. And there is a profound commitment to truth-telling and justice, displayed most powerfully in the work YTU has done to prevent harm and abuse and to contribute to repair and restitution for victims and survivors in and beyond the church.

As you read and reflect, celebrate and give thanks for YTU's past and present in this Jubilee Year, I encourage you to take a moment to consider where God might be calling YTU next in this time of renewal, and the part you might play in that journey.

The Origins and Beginnings of the Yarra Theological Union

PETER MALONE MSC

In those 'old days', seminaries were closed shops, self-sufficient. Each seminary, each order, had its experts, its Faculty. There was little exchange of lecturers. Seminarians of different religious congregations met each other rarely – and then it was often curiosity value; riding by bike to Box Hill to see what the Franciscan students were like, or a football match...

During the 1950s, there was encouragement from Rome for seminaries to look again at their curricula and move towards some creative developments. After all, the new information on biblical literature, languages and archeological sites meant an overhaul of scripture courses. Pius XII issued a document in 1956 that asked seminaries to use developments in education to assist in planning and re-writing courses.

Religious orders prided themselves on their seminary programs. But, by 1969, most congregations did not, in fact, have all their resources within their four walls. For one thing, the Vatican Council had asked for higher standards of theological education and had initiated so many developments in thinking and action – such a range of official documents, new presentations of Church law and a host of subjects relevant to the modern world that needed to be studied – that no seminary could maintain a complete and adequate staff.

When the Jesuits left their Sydney seminary at Pymble in 1968 and moved to some terraced houses in Melbourne, in Parkville, near Melbourne University and near the colleges which comprised the Melbourne College of Divinity and joined them, Cardinal Knox took an initiative for the diocesan seminary to become part of the college and the religious order seminaries to join as well. The orders had been feeling the need to share resources and, by the end of the 1960s, the different experts in particular areas were going from order to order giving their lectures – the Passionists in Templestowe, Franciscans in Box Hill, Carmelites in Donvale, Missionaries of the Sacred Heart in Croydon. This brought some freshness into courses in these years. Since the houses were in the eastern suburbs of Melbourne, they joined what was known as the Upper Yarra Consortium.

The Melbourne College of Divinity is an interesting institution in itself. It was constituted by an Act of the Victorian Parliament in 1910 and represented the Anglican, Baptist, Presbyterian, Methodist and Congregational Churches and, by co-option, the Churches of Christ. There were quite some developments in the 1970s. The Jesuits had joined with the Anglicans and the other Churches to form the UFT (United Faculty of Theology). Later, Methodists, Presbyterians, Congregationalists (with the exception of the 'Continuing Presbyterians') formed the Uniting Church in Australia and became a significant Church presence in the country.

Amendments to the Act in 1972 enabled the inclusion of representatives of Catholics and the Churches of Christ in the College. Also, in 1972, amendments to the Act enabled the College to introduce a degree over and above the Bachelor of Divinity degree they had been offering. The new degree was a primary degree in Theology, the B.Theol. (Bachelor of Theology). It was a degree to be taught by 'associated teaching institutions'. The degree was introduced in 1974, a significant move in ecumenical co-operation in the teaching of theology, with a qualification recognised by other universities. And, over the decades, it has led to further degrees and diplomas as well as a range of Masters and Doctoral programs.

However, the question of the early 1970s was the kind of affiliation Catholics should have with the College and how the associated teaching institutions should be constituted. The first question was whether the religious orders would accept Cardinal Knox's invitation to join with the seminary. At first, yes. Then, as religious orders are sometimes wont to do, no. They would form their own teaching institute. While some of the orders whose houses of studies were close to the diocesan seminary did, in fact, become part of what is still Catholic Theological College (CTC), those in the Upper Yarra Consortium decided that it sounded better to be called the Yarra Theological Union (YTU). In fact, with the Redemptorist students and staff leaving Ballarat for Melbourne at the beginning of 1972, the Consortium was getting larger but was still an arrangement which one might call a clerical 'gentlemen's agreement'.

Almost from the beginning, it was always a source of some confusion for some in the College – let alone mystified outsiders – about the use of acronyms: the MCD made up of UFT, CTC, YTU; and YTU itself incorporating OFM, MSC, CP, OCarm, CSsR. The SJs were in UFT while the OMI and SDB were in CTC. And later, when women religious became involved: SGS, RSM, CSB, RSC, SSS, OLSH, MSC (Sisters), PBVM, FMM and FMA. Those initials are for the different religious congregations (which could be Googled for further enlightenment or bafflement). But, back to the real task. What were we actually doing?

One of the interesting initiatives of the Consortium was to have the courses for the first year students of Franciscans, Passionists and Missionaries of the Sacred Heart (before their novitiate) together. One cautionary thought was that the students would lose their order's identity. Experience proved that this was never the case, despite three students in the early years moving to other congregations. Rather, identity was reinforced, often in a jingoistic, better-than-thou, attitude! – which needed tempering. This first year course was to include an introduction to theology, to the Old Testament, to the New Testament, Communications; and we travelled from campus to campus (comparing the relative merits of what was for morning tea, cakes, scones and – to MSC embarrassment – leftover breakfast cold toast. For students working together (rather than simply meeting for football matches or to hear an overseas lecturer, as had developed during the 1960s) there was now something substantial.

And this quickly developed. At the end of June 1972, classes were called off for three days and students, lecturers, formation personnel and some congregation leaders met to discuss the future of seminary collaboration. Discussions were heady. Butcher paper points and diagrams were imaginative. What followed is one of those minor miracles: the religious orders made the big step to forego independence and establish a theological union, to be one of the associate institutes of the MCD.

The decision was made that St Paschal's Box Hill, the Franciscan campus, would be the centre of the Union. It had the advantage of being closer to the city although accessible to eastern, north-eastern and southern suburbs. The name of the institute was far harder to come by, something telling but also something modest. Despite difficulties that many interstaters expressed, especially those from Sydney who thought that the Yarra River was so brown it must be flowing upside down, Yarra Theological Union was agreed on – and became a significant name for what is still a significant member of the University of Divinity (whose offices are now housed at St Paschal's). A first president of the YTU easily emerged – Humphrey O'Leary, a Redemptorist, and a surprising blend of Canon Lawyer and charismatic enthusiast. He led participants effectively through the process in June 1972 and, with infinite zest and patience, leading meeting after meeting, exercising a skill in diplomacy and attention to painstaking detail.

Then began some years of hard and constant – but fascinating – work. Staff were required to go to departmental meetings, faculty meetings, business meetings to look at traditional courses and see how they might be presented in the context of a theological degree. There was team-teaching, experimentation in lectures, seminars, tutorials, workshops venturing away from blackboards to overhead projectors, to pre-power point audio visuals (slides, music and so on) and film.

Ministry was a buzz word at the time. Part of the exhilaration was moving away from the drily abstract treatment of so many theological and moral issues. YTU did not want to be too academic in an ivory tower sense (though several lecturers were more comfortable there). There was a powerful desire to meet pastoral needs and for relevance to guide contents and treatment. Different types of assessment were tried – written and oral.

The bonds between the staff from the different congregations were important with so much time and energy spent in those meetings and discussions. In the late 1960s, besides the interchange of lecturers, lecturers met at annual Theology Conferences, a chance to compare notes, hear speakers, debate. Frequent meetings developed friendships and collaboration between the orders.

Teaching students from the different orders has led to friendships and collaboration in ministry ever since. The concerns of the formation personnel were also considered and so regular meetings were set up for what Tony Kelly, from the academics' point of view, used to refer to as the 'Formation Lobby', who were a support group, learning from the ways of doing things which meant dropping some of particular ways and adopting others.

By 1974, the Yarra Theological Union was ready to participate fully in the teaching of the Bachelor of Theology degree.

But by 1974, one of the main consequences of all these changes being in place was the arrival of lay students. Seminarians would not (and should not) study isolated from the rest of the Church. In February 1974, YTU opened its classes to lay students and a large number of sisters and teaching brothers. In fact, within a year or two, laity and religious would outnumber (and frequently out-achieve) the seminarians in each course. One of the features of YTU in its early days was the number of talented lay women who obtained their degree (often in long part-time work), went on to doctoral studies and became a more substantial presence in the Church. On television and in the parishes of the past, it may have been 'Father Knows Best', but the developments in wider theological education meant that this might not necessarily be so – and would not be so.

Lecturers received a modest stipend as an acknowledgment of their work. In the end, the lecturers at the time were substantially supported in financial matters by the religious orders themselves. The Provincial Superiors of the Congregations became the YTU Council.

By 1976, YTU was functioning well, the first graduates with B.Theol, sound collaboration with other members of the MCD, effective working together of religious, men and women, and lay students, women and men, encouraging prospects.

And, here we are, fifty years later.

Thanks to the contributors whose stories you will now read, taking us back to the then-past, the more recent past, and the present. One of the delights of reading these stories is to find quite a lot of cross-referencing to various staff members. There is the reminder that YTU began with the religious orders of men but by the end of the 70s there were women on the faculty, lay and religious, as well as in the administration. Many of the staff and students of the orders served as Australian Provincial Superiors on their councils. Some, men and women, were elected as Superior Generals and some to the General Councils. And many have taught theology internationally, from PNG to Rome, from Fiji to Nigeria. Five students are now bishops. Women have been elected to leadership in the Church. A present lecturer has been President of Catholic Religious Australia. And YTU has an Australian Senator graduate of YTU, Pat Dodson, Special Envoy on Aboriginal Affairs and Reconciliation.

Some of the 'bios' are longer than others – but they had distinctive stories and details which take us beyond the precincts of YTU. The memories remind us of their leadership in education, their publications – articles, books, theses – and membership of the Vatican's International Theological Commission. Many have been members of womens movements in the Church. Many of the Faculty have been members, some Fellows, of the various associations for Theology, Moral Theology, Scripture, Canon Law. Particular expertise has led to the establishment of the Heart of Life Centre, Spirituality and Pastoral outreach, Social Policy Connections and the Yarra Institute for Religion and Social Policy and, more recently, the Administration of the

University of Divinity's offices at St Paschal's, and the School of Indigenous Studies as well as for the National Council for Pastoral Research, an agency of the Australian Catholic Bishops Conference.

A tribute to those who exercised leadership

President
Christopher J. Monaghan CP (2009-)
Lawrence Nemer SVD (2008-2008)
Kathleen Williams RSM (2003-2007)
Thomas Knowles SSS (2002-2002) Acting President
Paul Chandler O.Carm (2000-2001)
Campion Murray OFM (1986-1993) (1998-1999)
Anthony J. Kelly CSsR (1981-1985) (1994-1997)
Jerome P. Crowe CP (1978-1980)
Humphrey P. O'Leary CSsR (1973-1977)

Academic Dean
Ross Fishburn (2013-)
Catherine McCahill SGS (2009-2012)
Gregory Brett CM (2004-2008)
Kathleen Williams RSM (1999-2002)
[Interim Academic Dean (2003)]
Margaret Jenkins CSB (1994-1998)
Mark O'Brien OP (1990-1993)
Joan Nowotny IBVM (1980-1989)
Peter Chalk MSC (1976-1979)

Registrar
Adam N. Couchman (2022-)

Janette Bredenoord Elliott (2010-2022)
Joanna Phua (2009-2009)
Rhosheen Meyers (2006-2008)
Kathlyn Moynihan (1976-2005)
Romuald Green OFM (1974-1975)
(With thanks to Katherine Blyth for the research)

And to staff who have died
Joan Nowotny IBVM
Margaret Jenkins CSB
Glenda Bourke SGS
Peter Price

Franciscans
Kevin Goode
Leo Hay
John McCristal
Campion Murray
Cormac Nagle
Angelo O'Hagan
Tom Murtagh
Theophane (Paul) Rush
Maurice West

Carmelites
Brian Pitman

Passionists
Marcellus Claeys
Jerome Crowe
Greg Manley

Redemptorists
Kees de Kuyer
Brian Lewis (former CSsR)
Laurie McCarthy

Missionaries of the Sacred Heart
Walter Black
Frank Fletcher

Jesuits
Arnie Hogan
Peter Kenny

Again, thanks to those who have contributed to this project celebrating fifty years at YTU.

> *Peter Malone, Missionary of the Sacred Heart, ordained 1965. Qualifications: History (ANU), Theology (Gregorian University), taught Old Testament Studies and Theology at the Yarra Theological Union and was a member of the staff of the National Pastoral Institute and the Heart of Life Centre for Spiritual and Pastoral Formation. He headed OCIC, The International Catholic Organisation for Cinema (1998-2001) and SIGNIS, The World Catholic Association for Communication (2001-2005), and has written several books on cinema, theology and spirituality.*

Fifty Memories

In the Beginning

MICHAEL A. KELLY CSsR

The 1960s is sometimes called the decade of revolution and even as a student at a boarding school I was aware many things were changing. It was the era of new music, especially that of the Beatles, who released their first album in 1963. It was a time of public protests, riots, and shootings at university campuses. Blue jeans, beards, body adornments, natural foods, drugs, gay marriage, and single parenthood gained acceptance. The hippie movement evoked a new era of sexuality and *Humanae Vitae* was the church's verdict on contraception. The Vietnam war was on our minds, especially when conscription was introduced. However, the biggest change for the Catholic community was Vatican II (1962-65). Despite the time the effect of the Council took to reach Australia, the winds of change were blowing.

Dioceses and religious orders had their own seminaries for the formation of ordinand candidates, but many departed ordained and religious life, new recruitments were modest, and there was a growing awareness that the future was going to be different. Religious leaders in the Catholic community looked at the possibility of pooling resources for formation and theological education as theology was breathing fresh air and the social sciences were part of the educational agenda. The first configuration of religious orders collaborating for theology in Melbourne was known as the Upper Yarra Consortium and seminarians would travel from one College to another each day for classes. The combined wisdom of those in charge was that we needed a centre and the Franciscans generously offered St Paschal as a venue. Fr Campion Murray OFM and Fr Humphrey O'Leary CSsR moved the nascent project in the direction of students being able to get degrees from the Melbourne College of Divinity. At the same time, there was significant dialogue with the bishops; and the diocesan seminary of Corpus Christi which had already changed location from Werribee to Glen Waverley and would move twice more to Mulgrave and then Carlton, tom become, eventually, the principal partner of Catholic Theological College. Religious were keen to preserve their exempt status in canon law so did not partner with the diocese.

After novitiate in Galong NSW and three years in the Redemptorist seminary in Ballarat, I moved to Kew and began to study at YTU in 1973. Initially, we were all seminarians but soon lay people began to study theology and I sought to ensure that I was in classes with lay people as they had more life experience than us young seminarians. Over a two-year period, the Redemptorists brought ten lecturers to the newly formed consortium, and they joined lecturers from other Colleges. In those early days, there were no degrees, but once the Catholic Colleges joined the MCD it was possible to graduate with a degree in theology and even undertake research degrees. Those who had completed several years of study had to enrol in YTU units but their completion of units was expedited because of what they had already studied.

The spirit of the 1960s influenced the mood of the 1970s, and in addition to formation in our religious communities and study at YTU and some of the other Colleges of the MCD, we were active in a variety of competitive sports as well as participating in pastoral work. After ordination in 1977, and ministry in Perth, Penrith, and Melbourne, I had the opportunity to study overseas. Building on my primary degree from MCD, I was able to complete two masters' awards and a doctorate. I have now been a student at YTU, a lecturer, a member of the Council of YTU as a provincial, and for two decades been involved in overseeing research and religious education programs at YTU.

The place has changed greatly and today many of those I taught are teachers who, in their workplace, influence the next generation of disciples and citizens.

I am grateful for the foundations given me at YTU and continue to be enriched by the faculty and students of YTU and the University of Divinity.

Michael A. Kelly CSsR teaches in the fields of practical theology and religious education. He has particular interest in the history and contemporary practice of religious education as well as in the fields of hermeneutics, preaching, leadership and the theology of ministry. His most recent publications include articles on preaching and religious education as well as a co-edited book.

Michael is also Research and Education Coordinator at Yarra Theological Union and a member of the Research Committee of the University of Divinity. He was on academic sabbatical in the second half of 2018, and, during this time, was a Visiting Fellow at the University of Durham.

Expanding Horizons

PAUL CHANDLER O.CARM

I arrived as a young seminarian to the Carmelite House of Studies in Donvale at the beginning of 1970. There were about twenty students in the community at the time. We had three teachers: a canon lawyer who taught philosophy and moral theology, a philosopher who taught scripture and theology, and a systematic theologian who was the only one to teach in his area of specialisation. We also managed a farm of about forty acres, with some dairy cows, about ninety pigs and three hundred chickens, with lawns to mow, hay to cut in season, acres of blackberries to eradicate, and wood to chop for fires, the only heating in the Melbourne winter. We looked forward – or rather did not – to six years of somewhat cloistered, self-contained life in small classes with the same people and the same improvising teachers.

But there was already light at the end of the tunnel. The clerical religious formation houses clustered in the Yarra Valley in the east of Melbourne were experimentally pooling their resources in what was first called the Yarra Valley Shared

Lecture Scheme. There was a slow beginning, but in the first year or so, I recall we travelled from Donvale to the Passionists in Templestowe to learn Old Testament with the formidably learned Bob Crotty and to the MSCs at Croydon to sit at the feet of Peter Hoy for church history. The larger than life Franciscan, John McCristal, taught us more church history at Donvale. A bit later, among other wonderful teachers, we had the Redemptorists Humphrey O'Leary for canon law, and the eloquent Tony Kelly for systematic theology. Cormac Nagle, OFM, taught us moral theology with a practical pastoral orientation, and Greg Manly, CP, memorably taught liturgy. At last we were being taught by experts.

Our small community circles expanded dramatically. There would have been some eighty or more seminarians all together. Our parties, barbecues and concerts were long and raucous, the stuff of legend. But it was an all-boy world, with much alcohol, many late nights, and an unconsidered Boys' Own misogyny, embarrassing to remember.

Within a couple of years, we ceased daily travel to settle at St Paschal's from 1972, through the extraordinary and long-lasting generosity of the Franciscan Friars. The first lay students arrived a year or two later. I recall that Barbara Hutchinson was the first woman student at what by then had matured into Yarra Theological Union, and, if I remember correctly, she was for a time the only woman student. The young male clerical world was crumbling, to our great and lasting enrichment. In 1973, YTU became a part of Melbourne College of Divinity, the award of degrees became possible the following year, and our horizons once again expanded.

I was ordained in 1975 and returned to YTU to teach in 1990, after some years of parish work and postgraduate studies in Rome and Toronto. There were some familiar faces – John McCristal still bestrode the history syllabus – but YTU had become a very different place, with a large, well-qualified, and varied faculty, all contributing their services. They were wonderful colleagues and YTU was run in a deeply collaborative way. Kathlyn Moynihan, the Registrar, held it all together with an unflappable calm and grace, awesome efficiency, and a remarkable institutional memory. There was a student body of some three hundred enthusiastic students, the vast majority lay people and the majority women. The average age had risen considerably, and there was now a maturity of reflection born of experience far beyond what there had been fifteen years before.

I soon realised that YTU was a dream teaching job. Students were there only because of a personal desire to deepen their faith and theological understanding. I marvelled at their enthusiasm and commitment. We had two sessions of evening classes, the first from 5:00 to 7:30 and the second from 7:30 to 10:00. I dreaded being rostered for the second, the late shift. It was about an hour's drive home and I would always be too wound up to sleep. But these night students were a joy to work with, as were all the others: keen, alert, thoughtful, diligent, engaged. And all this after working all day, cooking the family dinner, driving their daughter to ballet lessons, and coming out in the cold for two and a half hours of medieval church history. Teaching is always a learning experience, and I learned a lot in more ways than I could count.

It's fifteen years now since I reluctantly left YTU, and I still miss it. I consider myself blessed to have been part of it as a student and as a teacher.

Paul Chandler was born and raised in Sydney. He has been a Carmelite since 1970. After studies at YTU, he was ordained in 1975, worked in parishes for some years, and then did graduate degrees in Theology and Latin in Rome and Medieval Studies in Toronto, before returning to teach Church History and History of Spirituality at YTU from 1999 to 2016. He was President from 2000-2001. He is presently spiritual director at Holy Spirit Seminary, Banyo, Qld, and publishes on the history and spirituality of the medieval Carmelites

YTU – A Marvel of Improvisation

TONY KELLY CSsR

I am honoured to be invited by an old friend, colleague and film-critic Peter Malone MSC, to write these few words in appreciation of the immense theological contribution of YTU: we now have the beginning of an Australian theology – earthed in this time and space, alive to thousands of years of Aboriginal pre-history, and increasingly in contact with the ancient worlds of Asia, and caught up in new waves of missiology in Oceania. Many of the faculty belong to missionary orders involved in this part of the world, and hence brought a fresh sense of direction and a new breadth to the traditional business of theology.

It would be impossible to give any impression of the mood or texture of this time and without referring to key figures such as Humphrey O'Leary CSsR, Jerome Crowe CP, Campion Murray OFM, Angelo O'Hagan OFM and many others. They were all connected to the Second Vatican Council with all its creativity and ferment; and moved through times of rapid change, affecting religious orders, the Church as a whole, theology itself and theological education. These times experienced the trauma of *Humanae Vitae*, the influence of the different popes in this period, the opportunities and challenges of ecumenism, interfaith dialogue, and an increased ecological awareness. All this in collaboration with other venerable theological bodies, e.g. the United Faculty with its Jesuit membership.

All are especially indebted to Peter Malone, who, along with his highly regarded teaching and writing, flew the flag of expert review and comment on film at a time when that was not recognised by the prim theological establishment. Such hesitation must now sheepishly recognise Peter's international reputation in this domain. To sum up, YTU exhibited – in its curriculum style and expansiveness – a truly Catholic spirit, deep and broad, often in difficult times. That was a factor attracting many laity – especially teachers – into the study of theology, indeed, they went on to emerge as leaders in their respective fields – Anne Hunt, Marie Macdonald – to join with well-established authorities such as Sr Maryanne Confoy RSC as commanding figures in a vital area of faith-education and religious development. YTU in those years was a miracle of improvisation.

In some ways, YTU improvisation was grounded in diverse qualifications from Boston, Rome, Dublin, and other centres.

It is a special joy to have been part of this theological developments in education, and cultural awareness of the role of laity, women, and different religious orders. Some, like me, went on to other contributions through ACU, for example. But what has become clear is that YTU stands for enormous institutional and cultural change. No one can recall what it was like at YTU without recognising the powerful presence of Mrs Kathleen Moynahan and the colourful and omni-competent contribution of Sr Joan Nowotny IBVM

All in all, it was a privilege to have been able to contribute to one of the most significant developments in the Catholic community in Australia.

> *Tony Kelly, a priest of the Redemptorist Order. Doctoral and post-doctoral studies in Rome, Toronto and Paris. President of YTU for ten years. Formerly President of Australian Catholic Theological Association. Past Chair of the Forum of Australian Catholic Institutes of Theology. He was Head of Sub-Faculty of Philosophy and Theology at the Australian Catholic University from 1999-2004. In February 2004, he was appointed by Pope John Paul II to the International Theological Commission.*

Living in Times of Change

TOM MCDONOUGH CP

My own experience of shared theological formation began with classes with the Blessed Sacrament students at our Holy Cross monastery. The next year, we started a travelling Upper Yarra Consortium – Holy Cross one day, Whitefriars another, then the Franciscans. We settled finally at St Paschal's.

Those late 1960s and early 1970s were heady days, indeed. What a fantastic hope-filled, exciting time it was. After Vatican II, the winds of change blew like a gale. We had some of the best teachers in the church to stretch our minds and hearts. All we dozens of young men were going to change the world and change the Church. Far from losing our individuality, communion made us more aware of the unique gifts and spirit of each of our Congregations. Camaraderie, friendships, laughter, and the getting of wisdom, the excitement of theology, untold possibilities were part of the everyday in St Paschal's cloisters and in the classrooms

Jump a few years. I came back from studies in Louvain University to join the teaching staff of what was now YTU. Now the young religious men training for priesthood were joined by religious sisters and brothers working together, taking advantage of the B.Theol that YTU now offered. I doubled also as chaplain for the college. Our teachers now included women – Mary Scarfe, Sr Joan Nowotny, Sr Deirdre Brown, Sr Mary Reaburn, Sr Maryanne Confoy –wonderful women.

The number of seminarians grew as the Pallotines, Redemptorists, Divine Word Missionaries, Discalced Carmelites, Dominicans and others came to join the YTU family. Then, as numbers of seminarians and religious decreased, the numbers of men and women seeking personal and professional development grew. They came attracted by the unique, independent and prophetic voice of the Yarra Theological Union. They came for the depth and breadth of scholarship, for the sense of camaraderie, family and community that was and is so characteristic of YTU. They came because of the commitment to evangelisation and mission that underpinned the studies.

They came most importantly because they were attracted by the very deep and authentic spirituality of the college made up of the charisms of the founding congregations, and the stories of each of the students. This spirit and spirituality continues to grow in depth and breadth as the cultural mix of students and teachers changes, and as YTU continues to respond to the changing times we live in.

My time as chaplain, lecturer and member of the YTU community finished in 1990. Those early years were exiting indeed. We were taught by visionaries, great men and women who just saw themselves as servants of the Gospel. Following them as a teacher, I was humbled by their capacity to see and their courage to be the church the world needs.

Long may Yarra Theological Union continue the work.

Fr Tom McDonough is the current Provincial Superior of the Holy Spirit Province of the Passionist Congregation. This Province includes Australia, New Zealand, Papua New Guinea and Vietnam. Fr McDonough did his initial formation and training at what is now the Yarra Theological Union (University of Divinity) in Melbourne and then further studies in the Catholic University of Leuven (Belgium). He held a position as lecturer at the Yarra Theological Union for fifteen years. He then moved into parish and pastoral work in a number of parishes in Australia and Papua.

Memories of YTU 1972–1980

JOHN MULROONEY MSC

The first memory that comes to mind in 1972 is the daily commute! We MSC piled into 'second and third hand cars' and each day travelled to a different formation house – the Frannies at Box Hill; the Passionists at Templestowe and so on. The highlight of the morning was often morning tea. No-one could beat the Franciscans' hot jam donuts (the cold, leftover toast at the MSC's could not compete).

The teachers that spring to mind in those early days are people such as Walter Black MSC. He taught Moral Philosophy and I found his method of teaching was to my liking. He was clear, concise, logical and his class notes were outstanding and a great help to evening study and assignments. I was obviously enjoying the class because half way through the year he asked me to join the theologians moral group.

Another teacher was John Flynn MSC. He taught the 'Mystery of Christ' course. Very early on, we started to call it the 'Mystery of Flynn' course. It was quite some months into the course before Christ got a mention. He began with us reading some excerpts from literature, poetry, looking at art works/photography – helping us to get in touch with our own human experience and the experience of humanity. It was later we were introduced to Jesus in the Gospel of Mark and he led us to look upon and reflect on the humanity of Jesus.

I think that what made him a great teacher was the fact that he left us to make the connection/fusion between our own humanity and the humanity of Jesus. As a young fellow in High School, I had questioned the image of God as a 'little old man in the sky'. It did not make any sense to me. This course opened up a whole new way of seeing things and understanding the divine in the world and in humanity.

Thirty years later, I found myself a member of the YTU Council and Chair of the Council for a number of years. This gave me an insight into what a special place it is. The staff worked so hard (and often with minimum financial reward) to make it an intimate and special place for the students who attended. The fraternal relationships with other Provincials provided us all with an opportunity also to share about things other than YTU matters. I loved being part of all that.

Of course, there are lots of other memories through the years but these give us a small glimpse of the world of YTU in its early years.

> *John Mulrooney studied at YTU. In his ministry, he has been Principal of Downlands College, Chevalier College, Monivae College and has served as Deputy MSC Provincial and as Provincial Superior (2011-2017).*

My Early Years at YTU

ROSE MARIE PROSSER

YTU opened its doors to lay people in the mid-seventies and many, whose 'hearts were on fire' as a result of Vatican II teachings, enrolled in the night and day courses. The units were 10 point units as there were three terms rather than two semesters. In those days, just about everybody enrolled for a B.Theol.

When I started in 1977, Kath Moynihan was the Registrar and Jerome Crowe CP was President. At the time, my youngest of four children was just one year old. Many of the compulsory units were offered in the morning and in the evening. The evening lectures were from 7 – 10pm which gave family people time to have a meal beforehand. In my first year, I did three evening units as I had a very supportive husband who was able to look after and put the 7, 5, 3 and 1 year olds to bed. In those days, there were many seminarians, as well as the religious sisters and brothers, many of whom had been teaching for years, who were full of enthusiasm as they were now offered time to study theology. Most of the lay people were also teachers with university degrees so received some credit for previous study. I had studied science and had a PhD in Chemistry. Lay students were used to asking questions and discussing topics in class, which – for many seminarians – was a new experience. There was a vibrant SRC and, on at least one occasion, there was a 'Revue' put on in the theatre in the MSC monastery at Croydon. The many different religious orders were present with a large group of SVDs coming by bus from Essendon each day.

My first lecturer was Peter Malone MSC who taught 'Introduction to the Old Testament – the History of Israel'. Most Catholics in the 1970s had little knowledge about the Bible, especially the Old Testament. Peter gently nurtured us students into an understanding of the importance of biblical interpretation. In that first year, we had a new exciting young Dominican teaching Prophets – Mark O'Brien OP, just back in Australia after his studies in Rome. To teach, there was only really 'chalk and talk ' and pages of typed notes – as there were no overhead or data projectors!

We all had to take the three Church History units with John McCristal OFM. He was an older friar who had a distinctive white beard. He was a character. Anthony Kelly CSsR gave lectures with many 'flourishes' of hand. Leo Hay OFM taught many units, and had a style that contrasted with Tony Kelly's in that Leo was a person who stood at the lectern and spoke very calmly. Maryanne Confoy RSC introduced Religious Education as well as the unit 'Faith and the Human Lifecycle' into the curriculum The points gained for the Unit 'Liturgy: Formation in Participation' given by Tom McDonough CP could not be counted toward a B.Theol for laypeople!

So I give thanks for the gift that YTU has been to me – a loving, inclusive, non-clerical community, that values open and rigorous learning and teaching, and that has given me access to so much of the wisdom of our Catholic tradition. After many years in Catholic Secondary Education, I was fortunate to be asked become a lecturer at YTU and taught for 20 or so years in Practical Theology, teaching 'Faith, Religion and Spirituality in Contemporary Society' and 'Introduction to Scripture for Religious Educators'.

> Rose Marie Prosser taught in Catholic secondary schools, had a time in leadership at the Melbourne Catholic Education Office, worked with teachers in Catholic schools and then lectured at YTU for many years. She and her late husband Bob were Australian Regional Couple for Teams – an international Movement for Married Spirituality. She was a member of Archbishop Little's Pastoral Leadership Board in the nineties until it was disbanded when the next archbishop was appointed. She is presently secretary of Catholics for Renewal.

The Way We Were

PAUL BEIRNE

In February 1978, I pulled up the third-hand, VW Kombi van at the steps of St Paschal's Chapel, and nine young men tumbled noisily onto the tarmac. The Divine Word Missionaries (SVDs) had arrived at YTU! The first person we encountered was Fr Jerome Crowe, the President of YTU, whom we didn't know at the time. 'Ah', said Jerome. 'You must be the SVDs'. 'Yes, Father', I replied. Jerome looked us up and down, didn't add to his observation, and walked away. Looking at the motley crew in front of me, I didn't blame him. Our landing place looks very different forty-three years later. There was no Carmelite community at the entrance, no Dorish Maru; the retirement village was an empty field where we played touch football; the Franciscan printing press was in full operation with no hint of a Study Centre about it. The middle quad was alive with rabbits and guinea pigs, and there were a lot of seminarians belonging to a range of Orders in attendance

– Carmelites, Dominicans, Franciscans, Missionaries of the Sacred Heart, Pallottines, Passionists, Redemptorists, etc.

There were very few women students at that time. The first women novices arrived at YTU in 1973, and lay students enrolled in 1974, but their numbers did not match those of the seminarians. This mirrored a similar trend in relation to lecturers. Maryanne Confoy, Margaret Jenkins, Joan Nowotny and Mary Scarfe did truly outstanding work in their areas of expertise and were greatly appreciated.

That said, the list of male lecturers at the time was extensive by comparison: Tony Arthur, Walter Black, John Boyd Boland, Peter Cantwell, Jerome Crowe, Michael Fitzpatrick, Frank Fletcher, John Flynn, Kevin Goode, Leo Hay, Romuald Green, Kees de Kuyer, Tony Kelly, Brian Lewis, Peter Malone, Greg Manley, John McCrystal, Tom Murtaugh, Cormack Nagle, Mark O'Brien, Humphrey O'Leary, Brian Pittman, Frank Smith, Michael Tavuzzi and Martin Wilson – all of whom were also truly outstanding, pedagogically as well as personally. (I have listed both female and male lecturers in alphabetical order rather than by religious order as a sign of their solidarity and commitment to YTU. I suspect that this list is not exhaustive.)

In addition to seminary formation, in 1978 I undertook a bit of teaching myself, specifically, Peter Malone's *Mystery of Christ* (aka '*Mystery of Malone*') when Peter was away on leave. There were approximately fifty-five seminarians in that class, and just a few women. How things have changed since then.

An event that I remember fondly from those days is the Annual Student Revue where seminarians from the various orders, individually or as a group, put on skits that occasionally skirted just inside the margin of out and out bawdiness.

Segue to the present day. Things are very different now at YTU. Physically, the places mentioned in the first paragraph have sprung up, and the ratio of women to men is pretty even, faculty-wise, and in regard to students. The Church – and religion generally – has faced many challenges and it has changed as well.

However, what has not changed in all these years at Yarra Theological Union is a deep and united commitment to scholarly theory and praxis in theology, its related disciplines, and to religion generally, in coordination with the other Colleges of the University of Divinity. For me personally, it has been an enormous privilege to participate in this enterprise with scholars and friends who are a joy to work with, and to relax with. While I am looking forward to retirement, I know that I will miss this scholarship and camaraderie very, very much, and I am so grateful that I had the opportunity to play a minor role in its unfolding. *Ad multos annos*

> *Paul Beirne was a student at Downlands College, Toowoomba. He joined the Divine Word Missionaries and was a student director. He then went to Korea where he studied Korean religion. On his return to Australia, Paul was the Dean of Melbourne College of Divinity (now MCD University of Divinity), a position he held for eleven years. For some years, he was also Professor of Comparative Religion, with a particular interest in Asian spiritualities. From 2014-2021, he was the Director of the Heart of Life Centre for Spirituality and Pastoral Ministry.*

In Memory of Greg Manley CP Communicating the Experience of Liturgy

ANNELIESE REINHARD MSC

Greg was sent from Ireland to Rome to study, responded to a need in Australia for a lecturer in theology and later assigned to teach Liturgy – and the beginning of a journey of discovery and communication.

A first memory. Greg conducting Liturgy courses at the Blessed Sacrament Sisters community in Armadale to religious and pastoral workers. Memories say sleep and too difficult assignments, an academic experience, too heady for a young religious – rather reinforced with later images of YTU staff meetings, serious and venerable academics sitting in a circle.

A second memory. Greg teaching Liturgy at Assumption Institute to the women novices in the 1970s and asking me what I did with the novices instead of lectures and talks: just doing it, sharing... Greg began a profound change (and he said, at 55 not too late to change), disturbed by the atmosphere of the times, how he celebrated Eucharist, the experience of confreres leaving...

The third memory. Providing Greg with a book of images and getting him to write his personal responses opposite. My task as catalyst: how can we explain experience? By getting more in touch with experience.

The fourth memory. Greg and I at YTU. It seemed important to move away from the everyday atmosphere (like washing up cups and mugs in the common room). Important to create a setting, prepare some symbols and some beauty, and atmosphere, students not just coming in for a lecture with, perhaps, minds on the football grounds outside. At that stage, the seminarians' age and life experience meant they were ready to absorb knowledge, not so ready to be in touch with their inner selves. Many said they got nothing out of the Liturgy but Greg asked them whether it was important for them to get something out of pastoral work like visiting someone in hospital. It was the experience that was key. Another of his words of advice to the students who declared Liturgy was boring, 'unbore yourself'.

So Liturgy was part of the YTU curriculum but not just a subject or a course, but in those days for seminarians to experience being men first, to experience their humanness and bring that to their role as priests.

As Greg says in our book, *The Heart of Praying Liturgy* (Spectrum, 1984), pp. 5-6.

I had opened to me a whole new world: I learnt about the human person, human feelings, human development, and human relationships. I acquired the skill of reflecting, responding; I grew adept, not only in coming to a quiet in myself, but in leading others to come to it. I discovered the connection between liturgy and life, and new horizons in regard to presiding at the Eucharist. In those years, and not without a lot of dying and some suffering, I lost my fear of entering into the personal, the psychological world – although I did not recognise it as fear; I saw it as defending truth! I was changed; it was truly a conversion.

Anneliese Reinhard is a Missionary Sister of the Sacred Heart. Born in Germany, she migrated to Australia in the 1950s, teaching in the parish of West Heidelberg, studying Art, teaching at Christ College. For some years, she was Novice Director for her congregation. She has specialised in Liturgy, practical pastoral formation, working with Greg Manley CP. She studied in Chicago with Paul Robb SJ at the Institute for Spiritual Leadership and is a spiritual director.

Remembering Pastoral Counselling Courses

Mary Scarfe

I have sometimes wondered over the years about the long time I enjoyed teaching at YTU; how the material evolved so well and seemed to remain so interesting and relevant.

I took over from Father Peter Cantwell who was becoming ever busier with his Franciscan responsibilities. Peter knew my work well and the fact that he had confidence in me was very important to me.

YTU has always recognised and affirmed the knowledge, abilities and talents of women. Even from its early days, these were qualities of the institution which I must have recognised quickly. I obviously had some anxieties about being a layperson and female in the all-male, religious institution. However, the memory of my introduction is of being warmly welcomed.

I remember feeling at the time very sorry for the few students from overseas, as they were learning English as a second language, at the same time as trying to come to terms with the subject matter that they were studying. I am happy that, at YTU, this problem has now been addressed.

One of my first challenges was what to do about a difficulty I found in class: I tried to encourage group discussion, which was fundamental for making the material more real and for humanising theory into experience. This is something that current teaching method takes for granted, but at the time it was still very unfamiliar. Appropriate sharing in an intimate group setting requires an atmosphere of safety and I quickly became aware this was not present. The level of vulnerability it implied was not something most of the seminarians were comfortable with. Perhaps because it was not part of the culture, many of the seminarian students appeared distant and somehow a step removed from the discussion, as if it had nothing to do with them. They seemed even disconnected from their own lives and experience.

I could see how vital it was for them to be able to get in touch with their own feelings and become grounded in their own experience, if they were to become wise and compassionate leaders in their communities. It seems now that this was something the church's whole culture had yet to understand.

Looking back, I can now say that it was largely due to the inclusion of lay women in classes that gradually saw a shift in culture towards openness and collaboration. This is reflected in the gradual wider appreciation of religious and lay women and of their central role in the life of the church.

As more and more women were enrolling for my classes, they brought an added quality that comes from personal experience. They brought a level of comfort with interacting openly with peers on a personal level. It was through them that the atmosphere became real and safe.

I was particularly delighted each term when I saw the growing numbers of lay women in attendance lists. The women were enthusiastic students, whatever their own stories. Their presence and varied experiences, particularly with raising children, navigating the difficulties of daily life and with aging, had much to offer the young men. Many of the young seminarian had left their family environments to enter religious life. Some had missed out on being part of important learning events in their families, including the development of younger siblings.

Looking back over my thirty years at YTU, I think perhaps the course remained relevant because it was important in developing the attitudes and knowledge of so many religious and laypeople, many of whom went on to further study. The course encouraged self-reflection in a non-judgmental and creative way as an integral part of scholarship. It emphasised the necessity for self-knowledge before dispensing wisdom to others.

For myself, I am grateful because it deepened my own knowledge and understanding of being a therapist and trainer.

> Mary Scarfe was the first female member of the YTU staff. She studied at Melbourne University with qualifications in Counselling. For many years, she worked for the Catholic Family Bureau and then for the Anglican Bureau. Mary was also a supervisor in Siloam, the Spiritual Direction program at the Heart of Life Centre. She was part of the Teams of Our Lady and was involved with Women in the Church organisations.

Important at YTU

MARYANNE CONFOY RSC

In response to the question proposed by Peter Malone, 'communicator extraordinaire' and friend: 'What was important for you at YTU?', my first reaction was that this was too far down memory lane to even attempt to do justice to the request. However, on reflection, the fact that Yarra Theological Union, sponsored by male religious congregations, for priestly formation, made the radical decision to open courses to laity, men and women, interested in studying scripture and theology was of major importance to me. YTU was an institution that was committed to the values of Vatican II.

Another aspect of YTU that was important for me was the invitation I received to become a member of faculty there after returning from Boston College with my PhD. This was important because my interest was in the field of pastoral and ministerial theology. In my own teaching over the years,

I kept meeting people whose questions were about personal faith and belief in God.

The struggle to believe in God, the Church or even in the importance of one's own life was a reality in many post-Vatican II Catholics. But this search for meaning, purpose and faith was not confined to Catholics then, nor is it now. To use Roger Haight's terms for such quests in his contemporary studies of theology and spirituality: it was an issue for 'seekers, searchers and believers' across all walks of life and age groups. (Roger Haight, *Spirituality Seeking Theology*, 2016) YTU gave me the opportunity to offer my two key units in 'Faith and the Human Life Cycle'. My dominant focus was on psychosocial elements of adult religious development. I benefitted from the commitment of those women and men from varied backgrounds and expertise themselves. I was blessed by those students who enrolled in these units and enriched my teaching over the decades of my teaching at YTU.

The opportunity to work with colleagues was also important for me. The opportunity to co-teach a unit in Mystical Theology with Kathleen Williams offered an opportunity to collaborate, communicate and connect in collegiality. This meant that students benefitted from interdisciplinary teaching and research.

The commitment of students, their search for authenticity, for the connectedness of their studies with the reality of their lives within the community of scholarship offered at YTU was constantly important to me. My research was enriched by their questions and by the quality of their dedication and commitment.

The opportunity to supervise candidates for Master's Degrees and PhDs was also an important factor for me, as the topics these women were interested in pursuing were not necessarily catered for in the mainstream of the Academy. The first woman PhD to graduate from MCD, Marie McDonald, broadened the opportunities for women to engage in research topics which were educational as well as ministerial.

YTU was a place of academic studies, of scholarly research and of dedication to ministry and to service of the local and larger faith communities to which our students belonged. The blessings received by their commitments extended to the larger ecclesial community to which they belonged.

> *Maryanne Confoy is a Sister of Charity and has taught in primary, secondary and tertiary education in Australia and USA. She has worked in formation and given retreats and workshops for religious in USA, Ireland and Australia.*

YTU's Heyday

Stephen Hackett MSC

If theology schools can have a heyday, chances are YTU's occurred in the late 1970s and the 1980s. The number of religious institute students from the member colleges – seminaries, for want of a better descriptor – was still strong, if not as great as had been the case in the preceding decades. For the first time, religious women and brothers now had ready local access to theological education and enrolled in large numbers. And the number of laity choosing to study theology – whether for personal faith development, intellectual enquiry or for pastoral ministry – just kept growing. Most students were full-time, though when teachers from Catholic schools commenced theological studies, the number of part-time students increased.

YTU's enrolment through this period was perhaps the highest in its 50-year history. Yet that doesn't quite make for a heyday. But significant and complementary numbers of seminarians, religious and laity does, which served to create a climate for learning, marked more by a sense of Church than a consortium of seminaries. The men in initial formation from the member colleges, or at least some of them, probably invested more of themselves in YTU than did most other students; after all, they would be studying there for six or more years, on-and-off, which was longer than the religious and lay students whose end-point was a degree in theology rather than ordination.

There was a fine spirit of community, with the student common-room a popular and convivial meeting-place. For some years, an anthology of students' poetry was published, a mix of mostly serious poems with an occasional work of humorous rhyme. The Student Representative Council published a regular newsletter and supported a variety of student activities. There was a celebration for graduands with YTU offering congratulations to all who received the various academic awards of the then Melbourne College of Divinity.

The academic year began and ended with festive celebrations of the Eucharist in St Paschal's Chapel. On occasion, the Archbishop of Melbourne or the Apostolic Nuncio were invited to preside. The weekly celebration of the Eucharist was widely appreciated and well attended. Throughout the course of each year, YTU students participated in the celebrations of the perpetual profession of vows and ordination to the diaconate and priesthood of the mostly young men from the member colleges.

The course of studies for the ministerial priesthood, incorporating a Bachelor of Theology along the way, was a solid program of studies adapted from the traditional pattern of philosophy preceding theology to give significant place to the study of scripture from the outset. YTU had particular academic strengths in missiology and Catholic social teaching, which helped shape its outward-looking character. The faculty was comprised mostly of priests from the member colleges, along with a few religious and lay women. Some members of the faculty were experienced educators, others fine orators, and there were who some simply delivered the next lecture from their notes. A few enjoyed international standing. Some were widely published.

There were social occasions. An end-of-term (semesters came later) lunch at a nearby hotel always attracted a broad cross-section of students. An annual football match against a team from Catholic Theological College, then co-located with Corpus Christi College at Clayton, was characterised by YTU students, many coming from New South Wales and Queensland, bringing Rugby Union skills and tactics to an Australian Rules match. Every year wound up with the annual YTU Revue, an entertaining evening which showed off the talents of the students from the member colleges and others who chose to perform, while celebrating the bonds that existed within the YTU community, students, faculty and staff.

The YTU I remember from all those years ago is marked by friendships formed then which have endured through the decades since, and which continue to bring much mutual support and joy to life; surely an expression of God's loving kindness towards us. It was a time when the Second Vatican

Council was part of recent memory and still shaped our response to what was occurring within the Church and in the Church's mission in the world, along with the somewhat permissive 'spirit of Vatican II' which in hindsight seems to have been more limiting than liberating.

Of the men who commenced initial formation, relatively few persevered to ordination and, of those who did, quite a few subsequently left their religious institutes and resigned from the ministerial priesthood. Among the students and faculty there were a few who offended against children.

From both members of faculty and students who persevered in a religious vocation, some have been called to lead their religious institutes in Australia and internationally, while others have been appointed to the Order of Bishops. A number of those who were ordained have undertaken higher studies and then returned to teach at YTU or another theological faculty. Most have ministered among the People of God, both in Australia and beyond our shores.

Of the women religious and brothers and the laity who studied at YTU in its heyday, many have served in pastoral ministry in parishes, hospitals, and other places of ministry, as well as in leadership roles within religious institutes and major Church organisations. Quite a few undertook postgraduate studies and some later taught at YTU. The YTU of the late 1970s and the 1980s has become something of the quiet achiever, making its mark in the life and mission of the Church through its lay, vowed and ordained alumni. The Church has changed greatly during YTU's 50 years, yet it has adjusted to the changing landscape of theological education in Australia and has continued to engage innovatively and even prophetically to meet the needs of its students, the member colleges and their religious institutes, and the Church.

> *Stephen Hackett MSC studied at YTU 1978-1979 and 1982-1985. After attaining a B.Theol during his studies at YTU, he subsequently completed an M.Litt and an M.Ed, and a Ph.D with a thesis on the architecture of liturgy. Ordained in 1986, he has ministered in secondary education, university chaplaincy, vocations ministry, parishes, and diocesan governance. He is presently the General Secretary of the Australian Catholic Bishops Conference.*

YTU 45 Years Ago and Now

Sue Phillips FMM

I first became a student at YTU, forty-five years ago when it was a requirement of the formation program for the Franciscan Missionaries of Mary. Back then, the place was abuzz with many young seminarians, all dressed in their congregational habits, a wide array of flowing robes indeed. From memory, there were only a few young religious women to be seen and only one or two lay women on the teaching staff. There was a great spirit of welcome and inclusion, with the annual YTU Revue a much-anticipated moment to prepare and display all sorts of creative talent. To say nothing of the friendships that, unbeknown at the time, would carry through the decades.

In the FMM community where I was living, Barbara was the first woman to be studying for a B.Theol at YTU and we felt so proud. It is wonderful to know that, since that time, hundreds, if not thousands of lay women and men have followed, enriching the life of faith in the church of Melbourne and beyond.

In addition to taking classes at YTU in those days, we also followed a few subjects at the diocesan seminary in Clayton. The contrast could not have been more obvious. The quality of the lectures was to standard, but the atmosphere was more formal and less welcoming. We even sensed a certain hostility from some seminarians, objecting to women sharing their classrooms. Oh, how we loved YTU!

As I look back down those years, I realise that the spirit of openness and searching so present at YTU in its faith formation approach, laid a firm foundation for me. The drawing forth of inquiry and question, the encouragement to let go of firmly held beliefs and risk exploring other interpretations, broadened my understanding of faith, belief, church and Gospel.

I know now, with great certainty, that this early exposure to pondering, wondering, questioning, exploring held me in good stead. In later years, I was missioned to Morocco and lived the daily and all-pervasive impact of Islam. Then, more recently, I spent twelve years at the hierarchical centre of the church in Rome, with its own pervasive influence. In North Africa, my belief in the God of Jesus Christ was deeply enriched; in Rome, my loyalty to the Church was greatly challenged.

Both experiences profoundly affected me, calling me to question and reflect again on my understanding of God, on what does it mean to live the Gospel, on what do I really believe about the doctrines and dogmas the Church teaches, etc. I believe it was that initial formation in openness to these questions, that I received from my time at YTU, that gave me the confidence and ability to risk reviewing my own understanding in light of these experiences.

Returning to Australia and Melbourne several years ago, it was back to YTU. I went to enrol for audit. I immediately felt at home, hardly anything in the physical layout had changed, even the Common Room seemed much the same. The warmth and the welcome had definitely not changed, with even familiar faces from a long time ago. From all accounts, YTU's reputation for progressive thinking theology, policy and praxis was also unchanged. But change is there, in the demographic of the student cohort, with greater numbers of women and lay men, as well as believers of other traditions or none, reflecting the greater inclusiveness so necessary for our times.

Another important change that has happened in more recent years is the inclusion of the ELSPM (The English Language Studies Centre for Pastoral Ministry) program now sharing the YTU facilities. This initiative has been warmly welcomed by the FMM. We have had several of our sisters from other countries who have benefited enormously, not only from the English language study, but from the many friendships they too have formed.

Congratulations to all those who have contributed towards realising the founding vision of YTU and for its immeasurable contribution to the lives of us all.

Sue Phillips FMM was missioned to Morocco, North Africa, for nine years, before returning to Australia. She has been involved for many years in ministries accompanying people on the margins of society. In 2002, she was elected to the FMM International Leadership team in Rome and then for a further six years served as the International Leader. She is a founding member of Women's Wisdom in the Church Inc (WWITCH) and is currently involved in prison ministry.

A Reflection on 'My Students Days' at YTU

ANN LORKIN

I commenced my studies for a B.Theol. in 1981, having been granted a year of study leave from my full-time position at Siena College in Camberwell. After an emotional incident with my year 9 R.E. class, I had a serious chat with my principal, Sr Rosemarie Lewins OP, stating that you would not put a non-mathematician in front of a maths class and the same applied to RE teaching. Being 'a good Catholic' was not enough. I needed further study to be an effective faith communicator to young people.

My friend Rose-Marie Prosser had told me what a wonderful place YTU was to study scripture and theology and she was correct! As a fulltime student, I joined a vibrant community of staff, religious men and women, laity and young seminarians from the religious communities that formed the 'Union'. Completing the introductory courses in scripture with Peter Malone was exciting, having not long returned from a 'study trip' to Israel, Greece, Italy and France. As a geography teacher it all started to make sense in time and space likewise for the Church History units.

But I was there to master RE teaching and the bonus was Sr Maryanne Confoy, recently returned from Boston College with a doctorate in RE and Faith Development. Her evening classes for RE teachers were a demanding and exhausting exercise in knowledge and praxis. But so rewarding as new ideas, theories and insight were gained.

Being part of the community as a full-time student was rich and exciting. Lasting friendships were formed, especially amongst the religious women who took their study experiences seriously with such joy and passion. The freedom offered here was not to be wasted and their vision for the future in the church was infectious. On the home front, my husband had to look after the girls (8 and 10) at nights for evening lectures whilst at work explaining he thought I was studying theology not for finding new horizons but in a dead end as far as the church would be concerned. Forty years later, he is probably right!

During the next four years, I returned to teaching and studied part-time attending evening classes and weekend seminars. In 1982, I was able to have one day off to attend Church History lectures at CTC in Clayton. Here was a completely different community of diocesan seminarians, clergy and laity. Women were distinctly suspect and we felt out of place in the Common Room. The opportunity to study in other colleges was a wonderful freedom. I could choose locations, times and lecturers with expertise to suit my major areas of study. The year-long course with Rev. Denham Grierson 'Educating for Justice' at UFT completed my major in Religious Education and broadened my perspective significantly. I graduated in 1986 and obtained a new teaching position at Sacre Coeur advertised as a 'Full Time RE Teacher'. How much had changed over those years! A new professionalism had emerged and exciting developments were happening in our schools. One comment I heard in Sydney was that the Melbourne Archdiocese had more women theological graduates than it had ordained men! What an extraordinary fact and my response was what will they do with us? I went on to lead RE teams at Sacre Coeur and Genazzano finally having the title Faith Development Coordinator on the leadership team. Of course, I was not qualified to be chaplain. In retirement, I have used my skills in the local parish of Western Port at St Peter's in Shoreham and have links with the local Anglican communities and ecumenical spirituality groups.

My time at YTU was the catalyst for a rich and fulfilling life with so many faith companions on this journey. I give thanks for the staff – Fr Tony Kelly CSsR, Sr Joan Nowotney IBVM, the Religious Orders – Carmelites, Dominicans, Franciscans, MSCs, Pallotines, Passionists, SVDs and Redemptorists. Having studied with so many inspiring people was both transforming and life/faith affirming.

> *Ann Lorkin has taught in Melbourne Catholic Schools – Siena, Sacre Coeur, Genazzano. She retired to Shoreham and works in the parish of St Peter's and is involved in local ecumenical spirituality groups.*

Joan Nowotny: A Philosopher of Hope

BERNADETTE MICALLEF

When I think of my personal journey as a student at YTU over many years, two lecturers stand out for me. The first was Joan Nowotny.

In 1992, Joan had just finished her term as Dean and was teaching the methodology class for new students. Having been away from study for many years, I took this class. We connected immediately.

In my second year at YTU, I enrolled in Joan's basic philosophy classes, doing one unit each semester. The philosophy delighted my philosophical mind but it was the philosopher who taught me who made a deep impression on me. And classes were so much fun! The Dominican students would try to tease out of Joan extra clues for the regular cryptic crosswords she prepared for *Eureka Street*. Their efforts were to no avail but her evasion was much to the entertainment of the class.

Joan Nowotny: A Philosopher of Hope

Her classes were peppered with jokes. Illustrating a point in logic once, she told us of a person who enjoyed gin and tonic but found it left him worse for wear. So he tried whiskey and tonic and then vodka and tonic which had the same detrimental effect. Therefore, he resolved to give up tonic water.

I brought my then six year old son to class with me one day. He made his own notes and got a tick from Joan at the end of the class. She enjoyed later stories about him setting up a classroom complete with blackboard and chalk and teaching his teddy bears and assorted stuffed animals about 'physical events' and 'mental events'.

I did one more class with Joan on some existential philosophers and absolutely loved it once again. We heard about Joan's student days and afternoon tea with Marcel in Paris; about her 'soft spot' for Sartre; and Buber's 'I-Thou' relationships. Studying Marcel's intersubjectivity and the phenomenology of hope helped me understand my own experiences, and also the influence of these philosophers on Joan becoming the person that she was.

It was such a delight for me, years later, when I started driving Joan to and from the weekly Eucharist at YTU. With reducing mobility, she encouraged me to park on the grass as close to the door as possible. I pointed out the 'Do not park here' sign but her response was 'That doesn't mean us'. Apparently it did. we found out later!!

For three semesters, we had this little time together each week. I hoped it could go on forever but I knew this was not to be. One week I came to pick her up as usual but she wasn't ready. She'd forgotten. She looked tired and just old. I held her and kissed her and spoke my thoughts out loud. 'Don't die on me', I said. She replied, 'It's not far off'.

When first semester ended in 2008, Joan invited me to lunch at her place. This was the last time I saw her. She knew I was going on retreat that weekend and her last words to me were 'pray for me'. She died ten days later.

Sometime earlier, I had emailed Joan asking for prayer for a family situation. This was her reply.

> My dear Bernadette,
> Of course you will all be in my prayers.
> The Lord will take care of you and your family if you but trust.
> In love and hope, Joan.
> (What I do is live, how I pray is breathe.)

The 'love and hope' and the added afterthought on prayer reveals who Joan was, and who she was to me.

Bernadette Micallef is a self-declared 'perpetual student'. She began at YTU in 1992 after her second child started school. She now has a child older than she was at that time! After a very slow completion of a Bachelor, then a Graduate Diploma including the Siloam program at Heart of Life, in 2021, she began working toward the completion of the Masters in Spirituality.

Her work includes Spiritual Director at the Carmelite Centre, Melbourne, and also Planning and Website Assistant (www.carmelitecentremelbourne.org). She also works for the Conference of Spiritual Directors Australia as the Treasurer and Membership Co-ordinator. www.csdaustralia.com

Since 2006, she has also had what is effectively another part time job as the Financial Power of Attorney for her elderly mother who lost her sight at that time. Family is a big part of her life with three adult sons, two daughters-in-law, two grandchildren, many siblings and their families. She and her husband have one elderly parent each, both of whom are now in their 90s and in aged care. Life is, happily, very full.

YTU: Energising for Vatican II's Social Engagement

BRUCE DUNCAN CSSR

Yarra Theological Union in 1972 popped into the world, parented by the efforts of six or seven of the male religious orders. We Redemptorists had to relocate many of our 40 or so seminarians from Ballarat to Majella Court, Kew, when we joined that year.

In 1976, my Provincial asked me to focus on social justice ministry, and to study economics and politics at the University of Sydney. In 1986, I returned to YTU to teach in the social justice stream, and was delighted to find the College transformed by the large numbers of women religious and lay people among the students and staff. Many students were teachers, pastoral workers or professional people who brought their expertise into YTU which was abuzz with youthful energy and hopes for the Church.

As one of the first theological colleges to welcome lay students, YTU drew some 500 students from around Australia and parts of the Pacific. My confrere Fr Tony Kelly was President at this time, with a team of exceptional scholars like Cormac Nagle OFM, Jerome Crowe CP, Campion Murray OFM and, later, Larry Nemer SVD; and trail-blazing women lecturers, like Dr Margaret Jenkins CSB in Scripture and ecumenical dialogue, Dr Maryanne Confoy RSC in Pastoral Theology and Spirituality, and Dr Kathleen Williams RSM in Theology, later President of YTU.

As well as teaching units on justice and peace, I worked part-time for ten years with Catholic Social Services Victoria and was also a member of the Melbourne Catholic Commission for Justice and Peace along with Mr Peter Whiting until it was closed by Archbishop Hart.

Social Policy Connections and the Yarra Institute for Religion and Social Policy

However, to promote more independent and ecumenical social engagement, discussions began in 2002 and finally blossomed in March 2005 into the advocacy network – Social Policy Connections. It was funded by individual donors, religious orders and social agencies, along with member subscriptions. The SPC website at *www.socialpolicyconnections.com.au* finally went live in June 2008.

SPC did not claim to speak for the churches, but in its own name as an independent organisation inviting serious collaboration among people inspired by Gospel values. SPC drew from the traditions of social activism in the churches, including the writings and experience in Catholic social traditions, along with the scholarship, advocacy and commitment of the Anglican, Methodist, Salvation Army and Uniting Churches.

SPC had been in conversation for some time with the Melbourne College of Divinity about forming an ecumenical body for social research, which finally took shape in 2008 as the Yarra Institute for Religion and Social Policy (YIRSP). Following an invitation from the President of YTU, Dr Kathleen Williams, in August 2008 the Yarra Institute found a home along with SPC in the recently opened YTU Study Centre at Box Hill, along with the Redemptorist Social Justice Library.

I was appointed Director, with an eminent Board consisting of Dr Stephen Ames, Dr Rowan Ireland, Dr Paul Rule, Dr Robyn Reynolds and Drs Therese and Jim D'Orsa, along with Dr Wes Campbell later and Dr Peter Price. The Yarra Institute was formally endorsed by the YTU Council on 24 October 2008 and a *Memorandum of Understanding* was signed on 26 November. In the following ten years the Yarra Institute published eight books.

When the Melbourne College of Divinity morphed into the University of Divinity, discussions began about YIRSP becoming a research centre of the University. And so it was. In 2016, the new University of Divinity Centre for Research in Religion and Social Policy (RASP) was launched with Dr Gordon Preece Research Director.

Its mission achieved, in November 2018 the Yarra Institute cancelled its incorporation, with Stephen Ames and myself authorised to finalise any outstanding matters. YIRSP had achieved its initial goal. *Deo gratias.*

At Social Policy Connections, however, after operating for nearly two decades, its Board members recognised that SPC needed a younger generation and better resources to carry it forward. Initially, we opened conversations with prominent social and church agencies, but these efforts were scuppered by the consequences of the Covid-19 crisis, which hammered the staff and resources of all the agencies. After further consultations, the SPC Board on 20 November 2021 voted to close Social Policy Connections and to transfer remaining assets to a registered charity with similar objects. Peter Whiting and I were asked to manage the cancellation process, while keeping the website alive as an ongoing resource.

SPC is very grateful indeed for the wonderful way YTU and its staff welcomed and encouraged us over the years, particularly our president, Chris Monaghan CP, the Dean, Ross Fishburn, the Registrar, Janette Elliott, and the Admin staff Nicole and Katherine. You provided a home, support and facilities to help us along our way.

My special thanks are due to Peter Whiting who has been such a stalwart in helping shape and guide both SPC and the Yarra Institute over all this time, attending hundreds of meetings, chairing public forums, writing numerous monthly articles and editorials for the SPC newsletters and managing the financial accounts and business matters. His business skills well served his commitment to bringing Catholic social thinking to bear on today's troubling social problems and concerns. Always affable, we all greatly valued his diligence, insight and friendship.

Thanks also to all those, too many to mention personally, who have been part of this journey. What a joy it is to walk ecumenically together, listening carefully and learning from one another, breaking down walls and building bridges, as Pope Francis would say.

> Bruce Duncan was ordained for the Redemptorists in 1971 and later studied economics and politics at Sydney University. He was one of the founders and editors of the ecumenical social justice monthly, National Outlook from 1979-83. From 1986 to 2021, he taught various units at Yarra Theological Union on the history of Catholic social thought and movements in Australia and overseas, Marxism and Christianity, Liberation Theology, War and Peace, and economic development. He is chaplain with the Aboriginal Catholic Ministry in Melbourne.

From Friar Student to Guardian 'Landlord'...

STEPHEN BLISS OFM

It is a pleasure to have been asked to contribute to the anniversary of Yarra Theological Union.

I was a student of YTU from 1985-1990 with the Franciscan Friars (OFM), Minister Provincial of the Friars from 1998-2007 and then Guardian of St Paschal's from 2007-2010.

As a Friar-In-Formation, I loved going to YTU. I participated in classes for 6 years and gained the necessary academic requirements for priesthood within the Franciscan Order. I am quick to add that intrinsic to my formation was the interaction we were blessed to have with other students. I am forever grateful to YTU for it is ecumenical influences and the interaction I had with many female students and staff. These two aspects of exposure and learning have enabled me to be the Friar I am today. A consequence of this is the importance I place on collaborative ministry and inclusive leadership. I see graduates today from other institutions in parish ministry and in leadership and I cringe at their narrowness.

YTU exposed me, as did the Friars, to listen to women, seek their counsel and learn from them to live faithfully and credibly the Gospel life.

Several lecturers were very influential to me and helped form me in my ministry. Sr Margaret Jenkins CSB constantly challenged us to make sacramental theology relevant for today. I remember very clearly her challenge to us seminarians not to be afraid of being creative in ministry – I've heard her gentle and fun voice often in pastoral encounters I've experienced and this continues to empower me. Fr Peter Kenny SJ left an indelible mark of the importance of theological debate. Peter used to organise regular debates in the common room and we would form the 'pro' and the 'con' for a particular topic on Eucharist, Mariology, and other provoking topics. Sr Joan Nowonty IBVM would be the moderator and the SRC would host a social afterwards. I learned through these the importance of listening to others' opinions and that preparation is always essential to one's activity.

The YTU 'Revues' were loads of fun and gave us wonderful opportunities to perform, to work together and to learn how to organise a function. I was on the SRC for four years and was President as well. Sr Joan, being the 'social butterfly', loved the seminarians and provided us with many opportunities to enjoy and foster hospitality. Still now, the friars will often talk of those times with fondness and probably best to say what happened at the YTU Revues stays there! They are 'treasured' memories!

The suggestion from students to get a 'coke machine' stirred the student body up over many weeks and not only did we see the machine moved, it was replaced with the YTU Social Action Group whose role was to raise awareness of injustice within our society and Church. Many a time, one would walk through the Common Room and encounter a display which was more than thought provoking and was the topic of conversation over a coffee or tea.

Other people will mention the guinea pigs, and the rabbit, I'm sure!

Jumping a few years, I became Provincial Minister in 1998-2007 and served on the YTU Council and various Committees and in 2008 became Guardian of St Paschal's and once again a close relationship as the 'landlord'. It was in this period that the old Printing Press became more in use as a venue for Guest Speakers, etc. Whilst at St Paschal's, I was appointed Chaplain to YTU and we set up the St Clare's Prayer Room off the big Chapel.

I'm sure others will speak of the Chaplaincy role of YTU; suffice to say I enjoyed this appointment and it was an experience of accompaniment.

YTU has given me much, I'm proud of what I have gained from the women and men who have been students and lecturers. I am proud of all that the Franciscans have contributed to YTU, and I consider myself very fortunate that a large part of my formation was at YTU. it helped form me to be the minister I am today, and to have an inclusive understanding of Gospel living.

I humbly say 'thank-you' to all whom I've encountered at YTU over the last 27 years! My life has been absolutely enriched through my experience at YTU and the friends I have made over the years through various roles.

I pray YTU continues to have a wonderful future forming people for theological reflection and ministry and who are able to help reshape a Church which speaks for today and reimagines its expression into the future. In Francis and Clare.

> *Stephen Bliss was a student of YTU from 1985-1990 with the Franciscan Friars (OFM), Minister Provincial of the Friars from 1998-2007 and then Guardian of St Paschal's from 2007-2010. He joined the Ipswich Catholic community in mid 2016, having previously ministered in parishes throughout Queensland, Victoria, Tasmania and New South Wales. He also ministered to those in formation (at seminary) and in Administration of the Order. He enjoys parish ministry as it is an opportunity to journey with parishioners in their faith and for him to be inspired and challenged by their Gospel living. He tries to follow the simple way that St Francis of Assisi lived the Gospel of Jesus, and in his life give witness to the Franciscan values of joy, peace and respect.*

'Don't be smart; be helpful!'

ALOYSIUS REGO OCD

It is with great joy that I recall memories and make my contribution to this 50 years celebration of YTU.

I began my theological studies, in preparation for priestly ordination, at YTU in 1985, immediately after my novitiate with the Discalced Carmelite Friars. YTU was an unknown quantity to me, although I had heard some speak of this college in reverent tones as the best theological institution in Australia. Confronted with this knowledge and unsure of my abilities, I was somewhat apprehensive about coming to this place of serious theological study.

My first encounter with YTU was at the Eucharist for the commencement of the academic year. At this liturgical and social celebration, I met many new and continuing students and some staff members – and so, my first impressions were very positive, allaying some of my concerns. Many of the YTU alumni were ordination candidates from the various religious orders, and there were also some women religious and lay students.

YTU was blessed with some proficient and highly qualified lecturers. While most of the teaching staff were religious men from the various congregations constituting YTU, there were also some religious sisters (Joan Nowotny, Margaret Jenkins) and a few laity (Mary Scarfe). The lecturers were knowledgeable in their subject area and encouraged freedom of thought. The ethos at YTU was that of post-Vatican II theological creativity, preparing students for engagement with the secular world. At this time, the laity were already in the ascendant and the students from the religious orders were in decline. By the end of my studies in 1989, the lay students were, by far, in the majority. The lecturers challenged us to think, to ask our questions, and they supported us in our search. There were some colourful and eccentric personalities (Michael Tavuzzi OP, Angelo O'Hagan OFM) who had their unique and unconventional ways of teaching; there were others who were much more sober but no less stimulating (Campion Murray OFM, Denis Minns OP).

For me, there was much excitement and challenge in learning to think about my Christian faith. My childish and immature theological and scriptural presuppositions were being dismantled. And, at times, I felt that my faith was being destroyed; but, in fact, it was only being matured.

Studying with the candidates from the various religious orders was a boon. Friendships were formed, and we came to appreciate each other's charisms, and also to recognise how our own charism differed from theirs. Studying with the laity was also a blessing. These women and men brought some reality and normality into my rather sheltered and confined religious existence. They were also inspirational in the way they sacrificed themselves to engage in study of their faith. I returned to YTU in 1993 to begin post-grad studies. Again, this was a time of excitement and challenge, having personal supervision with some of Australia's most creative theologians: Philip Kennedy OP and Anthony Kelly CSsR These men challenged me to think hard and honestly, and to express myself clearly. Tony Kelly's sage advice: *'Don't be smart; be helpful'*, cut through the egotism of a young, would-be theologian, and has stood me in good stead in my preaching and teaching.

At the conclusion of my post-graduate studies, I joined the teaching staff at YTU. It was a real honour to be a member of this theological community. Teaching at YTU was one of the best preparations for preaching as it forced me to listen to the real questions and issues of the students, to explore answers, and to formulate honest, coherent responses.

I am grateful to YTU and am proud to be considered an alumnus of this theological institution. I wish YTU every blessing for the future and pray that its commitment to good theological education may continue and prosper.

Aloysius Rego migrated with his family from Burma (Myanmar) in 1969. After finishing his secondary and tertiary studies in Sydney, he worked for 3 years as an engineer. He joined the Discalced Carmelite Friars in 1983, began his undergraduate studies at YTU in 1985, and was ordained to the priesthood in 1989. In 1992, Aloysius returned to YTU and commenced postgraduate studies through the Melbourne College of Divinity. Having completed his postgraduate studies, he joined the teaching staff in the Department of Theology and Church History at YTU from 1998-2005. Aloysius has served his Order in roles of leadership and formation. His main area of work has been in retreat ministry. He currently resides at Mt Carmel Priory in Varroville (NSW).

Feeding the Soul's Hunger

MARY COLOE PBVM

I turned up at YTU in 1984 and then plodded through my B.Theol (Hons) until 1993. I say plodded as most of my study was one unit a semester, after a day's teaching. I remember packed to overflowing classrooms in those early years as lay men and women were finally allowed into theological studies – and we swarmed in! Many of us were teachers who had not had a chance to do serious theology, and each class was a revelation – and a revolution, as previous religious certainties from primary school were challenged and some tossed aside. Many of the women students were members of religious congregations from around Australia and life-long friendships were made. At first, there were some objections to women attending classes, lest the 'standard' drop. A quick look at final grades and the high distinctions earned by women, appeased that anxiety, and raised new challenges.

Our lecturers were not much older than ourselves, freshly minted from their higher studies overseas. And our lecturers make a list of 'who's who' in Australian Theology. Their names frequented our bibliographies – Tony Kelly, Mark O'Brien, Angelo O'Hagan, Frank Moloney – at that early time there were few women who had been permitted to study higher degrees in theology; Mary-Anne Confoy was a notable exception and her classes were very popular.

I remember animated classroom discussions. The students were a very mixed group and no presumptions could be made about background or faith, and there were no topics that were 'unquestionable'. Students wanted answers, and could not accept theological 'jargon' in place of clearly thought-out propositions that had their own authority in intellectual rigour – and, of course, the personal testimony of a life lived from that place of faith. And yes, during those turbulent years, we acquired the nickname of 'heresy hill', due I'm sure to our location in Box Hill – as well as an openness to new thinking and challenge. It was a place where the call of Vatican II was being met within a rich heritage of Catholic intellectual strength. YTU fed my inner 'soul' hunger.

Back then, essays were typed, and if you dared use Greek or Hebrew, then you guessed the space you needed to leave to write this in by hand. Guessing was also required for the space to leave at the bottom of each page for footnotes – either that or cite all references as endnotes. This was study without computers, no world wide web, no google or online databases. When I was searching for information, it meant travelling to the library and looking up cards in a catalogue, then books on shelves. It was slow, painstaking, work!

Then in the 90s I was able to begin a doctorate. At this point, my bibliography became a list of my teachers, mentors and friends, and I was introduced to an Apple! In the 90s, the internet began and it became possible to send an article to someone overseas using file-transfer-protocols. Later, this became much easier with the world wide web. The typewriter made way for a computer with 4 kb memory that could be expanded to 8 kb!

YTU strengthened my teaching skills as it provided a firm foundation for daring to teach Religious Education in the post-Vatican II world. With my YTU teachers as models and mentors, I engaged with my secondary students with greater freedom, certainty and the confidence to say – 'I don't know the answer to that question; I'll need to think about it'. Having a doctorate took my teaching into the tertiary world in Australia and overseas. Research and writing became a way of life alongside teaching.

So now, I have come full circle. I've returned to YTU, as teacher, author, and research supervisor. I trust that I continue to model the faith and intellectual integrity of my past lecturers in the ongoing exploration of the great divine and personal, Mystery.

Mary Coloe is a Presentation Sister, teaching at YTU since 2014 primarily in New Testament. Before this, Mary taught in both primary and secondary schools and then over twenty years at ACU. She completed her doctorate on the Gospel of John in 1999. Mary has taught New Testament studies in Melbourne and at the seminary in Brisbane. She has also taught at Boston College, the Jesuit School of Theology, Berkeley, and in Jerusalem. In 2013, Mary was invited by the Pontifical Council for Christian Unity to participate in a six year international dialogue between the Catholic Church and the Church of Christ.

YTU – Fond Memories and Heartfelt Thanks

ANNE HUNT

I have the fondest memories of my time as a student at YTU in the 1980s.

I was a teacher of Science and Mathematics and, having just concluded some studies in Education, I enrolled at YTU, thinking that it would be interesting to know more about Church history and doctrine.

As a part time student, it would take five years, attending classes, mostly two nights per week, to complete the Bachelor of Theology. There were many other school teachers like me in the student cohort. In those days, although having bachelor degrees in other areas (for me, that was Science), we enrolled in a second bachelor degree without question.

From my very first class, I relished the lectures, the ideas they raised, and the explorations they prompted.

Coming from a Science/Mathematics background, I was trained to write scientific reports, writing succinctly in 'past tense, passive voice'. Writing essays was quite new for me. But my lecturers were patient as I gradually learnt what to do and how to approach essay writing. Nor was I used to classroom discussion. There was none of that in a Chemistry lecture.

I recall many fine lecturers and wonderful teaching over my years as a student at YTU, including Peter Malone (my very first lecture), Michael Mason, Tony Kelly, John McCristal, Campion Murray, Kevin O'Shea, Mark O'Brien, Maryanne Confoy. Years later, when pursuing further studies in USA, I realised how very blessed we had been.

I fondly remember Joan Nowotny, Academic Dean, who was always so warm and welcoming; and Kath Moynihan, Registrar, always so helpful and reliable. The library was a great resource and the librarians unfailingly generous in assisting and advising us.

I remember many delightful fellow students, lay and religious, learning together. We would always enjoy a mid-lecture tea break in the common room. There was a lot of laughter and camaraderie. Classes were full. Guinea pigs sometimes popped in on lectures. I still smile when I recall our gales of laughter when Fr John McCristal spoke of the Stylites providing well-balanced advice. There was a great spirit in the YTU community.

I relished the teaching and the learning, right from my very first class. I loved deep-diving into the scriptures; the theological explorations into the mysteries of our faith; the highs, lows and controversies in Church history and how our Christian faith and doctrine took shape and developed. I especially loved learning about developments in the early Church.

The intellectual engagement with it all, in the milieu of a lively faith community that was YTU, was stimulating, nourishing, challenging and enlightening. Looking back, I see that YTU had a great influence on me, informing, reforming and strengthening my faith in my journey of 'faith seeking understanding'.

I am still seeking understanding! After completing the bachelor degree, I pursued further studies in theology. Several years later, I was privileged and pleased to return to YTU to teach a unit each year. It was a treat to return to the YTU community and to enjoy again the warmth, hospitality and spirit that is so much a part of YTU.

Hearty congratulations and thanks to YTU for all that it has achieved and for all that it has contributed to the Church in myriad ways, seen and unseen, in the fifty years since its foundation. All praise and thanks to those visionary founders of the Union in the 1970s, and to all who have continued to support and nourish it over the years.

> *Anne Hunt was a student at YTU in the 1980s. She later undertook further study in USA, then completed a Doctor of Theology degree under the auspices of the Melbourne College of Divinity (now the University of Divinity). She taught as a sessional lecturer at YTU from the mid-1990s to the mid-2000s. Anne served as the President of the Australian Catholic Theological Association.*

Memories of my Alma Mater YTU

VINCENT LONG OFM CONV

I was a student at YTU during 1984-1990. We, Conventual Franciscans, were the Johnny-come-lately to the Union. Prior to coming to Melbourne, our students for the priesthood had studied at Hunters Hill, Sydney.

I was fresh out of the novitiate and found formal studies quite daunting. The years of disruption following the Fall of Saigon and the refugee experience did not help. Nevertheless, I found myself gradually adjusting to the rigour of academic discipline alongside many other fellow religious men and women. The campus was surrounded with formation houses of congregations such as Franciscans, Divine Word Missionaries, Missionaries of the Sacred Heart, Redemptorists, Blessed Sacrament, Discalced Carmelites, Dominicans, Passionists and others. The network of friendships that were formed during those years would have a long-lasting impact and stand me in good stead.

I enjoyed the supportive, diverse and inclusive culture at YTU. Its small size overall made it easily a tight knit community where we all knew each other, staff and students. Quite unlike the seminary atmosphere I had experienced in my native Vietnam, we students thrived on the open, collaborative and engaging environment. Lay, clerical and religious alike enjoyed opportunities for learning, interaction as well as non-curriculum activities.

It has been more than 30 years since I left my Alma Mater. My life journey has since taken many twists and turns, including a stint in Rome as a General Councillor and now a bishop in one of the most diverse regions of Australia. I always look back with gratitude and consider my formative years at YTU as being foundational to my growth as a Franciscan, a priest, a bishop but most of all a human being and a fellow pilgrim with others. I am indebted to the lecturers, staff and students – some have preceded us – with whom I was privileged to have shared the journey.

Ad multos annos!

> *Vincent Long OFM Conv. was born in Vietnam and migrated to Australia in 1979 (including 16 months in a refugee camp in Malaysia). He entered the Franciscan Conventuals and was ordained in 1989, served as the Australian Provincial Superior, then as a General Councillor in Rome. He was ordained Bishop in 2011, serving as an auxiliary Bishop in the Archdiocese of Melbourne. He became Bishop of Parramatta in 2016.*

YTU Theological/Pastoral

TIM NORTON SVD

Towards the end of my theological studies at YTU, I had a part-time job as a physiotherapist in what was then Pentridge Prison. (I had studied physiotherapy prior to joining SVD.) Although I was genuinely surprised at the number of violence-related injuries I was treating, I enjoyed this work, and believed I was contributing to the mission of God in the world through these physiotherapy sessions.

On one occasion, I was asked to treat a prisoner in solitary confinement. As I was given entry to his cell, one of the prison guards accompanying me told me to make sure I 'hurt' the prisoner while I was treating him. I was confused by his suggestion. The man I was treating had recently been hospitalised after a severe beating by other prisoners. He had significant, ongoing pain in his neck and shoulders. This was the reason I was asked to treat him.

I gently worked on his cervical spine as he lay face down on the treatment table. And, as very often happens during treatment sessions, he began to tell me his story. He spoke of a traumatic childhood with regular physical and sexual abuse. As an adult, he became a substance abuser, and had no significant relationships in his life. He then told me that he was in prison because he had abused two children.

I found myself becoming increasingly uncomfortable as I attempted to heal a man who had hurt children. As I drove back to the seminary that afternoon, I wondered if I was actually doing something unethical by treating this guy.

The following day, I went to a class at YTU in systematic theology. I was still feeling very uneasy about the treatment session the previous day. As the class progressed, I summoned the courage to raise my hand to explain to the lecturer the situation I was facing. He immediately told all my class-mates to close their books. He then asked us all to think about this situation and discuss the ethical issues that it raised. He conducted what was for me an enormously helpful open conversation. There were members of the class who made a case that I should discontinue the treatment on moral grounds, while others encouraged me to continue, saying that we are all sinners. We talked about church doctrine as well as moral and biblical considerations.

We did not come to any specific conclusion; however, I returned to the prison much clearer on my position to continue providing treatment to that prisoner. After all, if I was going to treat people with conditions attached, then I should be doing something else. This was a very good example of the deeply practical and compassionate approach to theological studies that YTU provided.

Many years later, as Provincial of the SVDs in Australia, New Zealand and Thailand, I was elected the vice chair of the YTU Council. This was a very short-lived position as the chair was appointed a bishop. Thus, I moved into the position of chair. Although not particularly comfortable in such a role in a theological institution, I was encouraged by my peers (provincials, administration staff and lecturers) to remain in that position for three years. I was privileged to see how such an institution operates from the inside.

I was involved in planning, funding, conflict management, employment processes and facilitation. Yes, it was a considerable amount of work. However, the creativity, commitment, professionalism and good humour that I encountered sustained me and was a testament to YTU. I was also very aware of the significant extra work that YTU staff members were doing in favour of the increasing number of SVD students who were studying there with English as their second or third language. This effort produced outstanding results among our students, and they left the institution with a very high regard for YTU. Winners all around!

> Originally from suburban Ryde in Sydney, Tim Norton was trained as a physiotherapist and worked with young street people in Darlinghurst who were experiencing homelessness, addiction and mental health issues. He joined the SVDs, studying in Melbourne and Mexico, 1986. He was ordained in 1991. After six years working in formation in Melbourne and Sydney, nine years as the SVD Australian provincial, he spent seven years in Nemi Retreat Centre just outside Rome managing the society's renewal programs for priests and brothers. In 2021, he was appointed an auxiliary bishop of Brisbane.

YTU Fifty Years – an SVD Reflection

MICHAEL HARDIE SVD

The Divine Word Missionaries' decision in 1985 to build a house of formation at Box Hill, Victoria, on a leased section of Franciscan property and immediately adjacent to the present YTU campus, has been seen in succeeding years to have been a wise and far-reaching one. Although not without criticism in those days due to the dearth of local vocations, the SVD provincial at the time, Father Peter O'Reilly (now deceased) explained the decision in terms of utility: that living next to YTU, just 5 minutes from classes, would have a time-saving advantage for SVD students compared with the time-consuming daily journey to and from the then existing SVD house at Vida Street, Essendon. Peter got his way, and by 1988 a new SVD formation house – Dorish Maru College – was up and running. When I joined the SVD in 1989 and began my formation studies in 1990, there were six of us in community including the newly-arrived Dr Larry Nemer SVD, who was to remain closely associated with YTU in both lecturing and academic administration until his final days.

Across the span of YTU's remarkable 50 years, SVD missionaries and academic lecturers have been fortunate to have been invited to contribute to the curriculum. The connection with the wider SVD has enabled YTU to offer specialised units in mission studies including missiology, cross-cultural theologies and anthropological missiology units delivered by lecturers such as James Knight, Ennio Mantovani, Steven Bevans and Jacob Kavunkal – to name a few whose classes I have attended – with Albano Da Costa currently lecturing in the Theology of Mission.

Although it is true that we have not yet recovered from the downturn in local vocations in Australia, none-the-less the SVD formation house at Box Hill has always had a full complement of students, coming from across the SVD world to do their formation and higher studies at YTU. During my own time of studies for priesthood (1990 to 1996), I shared the house with other hopefuls from a number of countries including Vietnam, Indonesia, Ghana, the islands of the Pacific, Angola and the Philippines: all drawn to the YTU campus on the basis of the quality of the units on offer, together with the reputation of YTU as a great teaching/learning community. Such a reputation has come not only from the dedication to academic excellence, but also from the social experience of the Common Room, where students and staff could always be found mixing together informally during the class breaks – often a surprise for students from more conservative, overseas cultures!

My experience as a student of theology during my time of formation at YTU has been distinctly positive and affirming of the call to the vowed religious life. The units I chose, the qualifications I gained and the lecturers I engaged with, prepared me for mission and ministry in Vietnam in ways that no other academic institution could have done. One reason for this, I propose, was that each and every unit of study contained a spiritual component: in addition to the academic learning, there was always the dimension of the holy, fostered by the spirituality of the lecturer, leading the inquirer along paths to the sacred as the unit progressed. To this day, I still draw upon the spiritual wisdom of my past lecturers and guides, even if academically I've forgotten a few things!

Following from the years of study, and the aching over assignments and deadlines, has come a singular understanding – the value of the concept of life-long learning. After 14 years in mission in Vietnam, upon my return to Melbourne in 2012, the first thing I did was to head for YTU and enrol in yet another Masters course. In my desire for higher studies, I found myself naturally turning to my old Alma Mater as a continuing inspiration for further research and development. Today, although my time of formal studies has passed, I look back fondly and gratefully to those halcyon days of academic endeavour that have shaped my life as a Divine Word Missionary.

> *Michael Hardie, Divine Word Missionary, studied at YTU and spent 14 years in mission in Vietnam, from 1997 to 2011. He is now the JPIC (Justice, Peace and the Integrity of Creation) Co-ordinator for the Australia Province, and the Director of Professional Standards and Safeguarding.*

Part of the YTU Community

Mary Reaburn NDS

It has been a joy to have been part of the YTU community for most of the 50 years we are celebrating, first as a student and then as a lecturer. I am pleased to share some memories of wonderful women associated by YTU's story.

First, let me say that *community* is the word I associate with YTU, an inclusive community, a wonderful mixture of the most extraordinary people. Students from many parts of the world, who bring the riches of their cultures. Staff who always put the students at the centre of decision-making. In the early years, the students in day-time classes were mainly preparing for priestly ordination and those in the evening classes were generally teachers and parishioners wanting to grasp the best of the church's tradition. Today, even this has changed.

I want to reflect on some marvellous women who helped keep YTU going. I remember Kathlyn Moynihan who was the first lay Registrar, an Irish woman, who was always welcoming and helpful yet who also had high standards which were to be maintained! She gently explained until students and staff complied. Kath's first office was in St Paschal's library. Later her office was moved upstairs to the present-day Registrar's office. Kath was the go-to person for any question and for anything needed: first aid, sheets for the overhead projector, chalk, a class list. She did all this while maintaining the records and fulfilling the Registrar's responsibilities with care and precision. If a different type of job needed doing, Kath would get her husband, Jimmie, to come in on the weekend and do the task. I know that the shelf covering the basin in my current office was built and painted by Jimmie.

I remember too Joan Nowotny, the first woman to be Dean. Joan, a Loreto Sister, was a character, full of laughter and fun. Joan welcomed students to YTU and helped them find their way both in their studies (her job) and into the community of YTU. Joan taught Philosophy and loved words. She created cryptic-crosswords for the magazine *Eureka Street* and was paid with a box of red wine twice a year.

Mary Scarfe was, as far as I remember, the first woman to lecture at YTU. She was a psychologist and taught with Peter Cantwell OFM for many years. I remember too Margaret Jenkins CSB who taught Systematic Theology. Margaret was an extremely astute woman; she saw what was needed and generously contributed. For many years, she prepared the setting for the end of year Faculty dinner, at the Pallotines and later at the Redemptorists. Margaret had a special love for the work of Yves Congar and his approach to theology but she introduced her students to a range of methods, ways of thinking theologically, and theologians. She always wanted her students to find their theological interests. Later, the number of women on the Faculty of YTU increased and they were always welcomed by the mainly clerical faculty. I remember being the only woman in the Biblical Studies and Church History department. My first department Dinner was quite an experience. Dinner out with seven or eight priests. I heard later that they arranged seating so that I was not facing the men's toilets. Such thoughtfulness was appreciated and made me smile.

The pattern of women and men, laity and clerics, working to create community has continued to define YTU up to today. In this community of faith, we seek to understand, to ask questions and to search for answers together.

Mary Reaburn teaches Wisdom Literature and Psalms. She is a Sister of Our Lady of Sion and has a deep respect for the literature we call the Old Testament or First Testament and for Jewish and Christian interpretation of these texts. She has also taught at Holy Trinity Theological College in Harare, Zimbabwe. She is member of the Council of the Australian Bishops' Conference for Christian Unity and Inter-religious Dialogue and on the Ecumenical and Interfaith Commission of the Melbourne Archdiocese. She is particularly involved in Jewish-Christian and Jewish-Catholic relations. Mary has spent time in Jerusalem in conjunction with the Biblical formation programs offered by the Sisters of Our Lady of Sion at Ecce Homo Convent.

An Appreciation of Yarra Theological Union on its 50th Anniversary

MARK O'BRIEN OP

YTU's 50th anniversary is not only an opportunity to celebrate a remarkable milestone but, perhaps even more importantly, to give thanks for the untiring commitment of those who work there or have worked there. Except for occasional circumstances beyond its control – such as the recent Covid crisis – YTU has had its doors open and successfully provided ongoing service to students and staff, as well as the general public, for half a century. A remarkable achievement, especially when one takes into account that it is not constituted as a business, does not have its own premises but operates in ones kindly provided by the Franciscan Friars, and relies more on the personal commitment of its staff than financially lucrative contracts.

YTU has never been in the money game. In my judgment, a group within YTU to whom we owe a particular debt of gratitude is the administrative staff of the various Registrars and their assistants. As a lecturer, I come to give my classes and then go; I am an itinerant whereas the Registrars and their assistants always have to be there and are always there to assist the likes of me.

The first Registrar was the Franciscan Friar Romuald Green, who got YTU off to a great start, ably assisted by his secretaries. He was succeeded by a remarkable pair in Kathlyn Moynihan as Registrar and Estelle Pratt as her Secretary. I had the benefit of working with them during my three years as Academic Dean from 1990 to 1993 and always enjoyed listening to Kathlyn's rich Irish accent. Being an administrative low life, I was deeply impressed by their ability to respond to the different groups at YTU and the unique individuals in each group, and to meet their needs and desires in a professional and very Christian manner—students and staff, academics and administrators, the different religious orders involved in YTU. They did this over a considerable number of years, always with the aim of making a positive contribution to the Church and the wider Australian society. I was not able to continue lecturing at YTU after my time as Dean and so missed experiencing the valuable contributions of those who succeeded Kathlyn and Estelle, namely Rosheen Meyers and Joann Phua as Registrars, with Carolyn and Katrina Sombekke, Jean Gaydor-Whyte, Julie Binstead, and Hayley Alexander as secretaries. They continued the great work of their predecessors and were in turn succeeded by Janette Bradenoord-Elliott as Registrar, with Nicole Ross and Katherine Blyth as assistants. These have operated as YTU's administrative team to the present day and this has been a blessing for all of us.

Janette and her assistants had to deal with a marked change in the structure and operations of YTU when the Melbourne College of Divinity, to which it was earlier affiliated, became the University of Divinity, Melbourne. As expected, this involved some changes to the structure of awards granted by the University, the number of points awarded for completed undergraduate and graduate units, and the overall number of points required for awards and their distribution across the major theological disciplines. More recently, YTU has also enhanced its contribution to the awards the university grants to teachers in Religious Education in Schools. Janette and Nicole and Kathryn have worked closely with the President, Academic Dean and Faculty of YTU to implement these changes in a professional manner. It is because YTU has benefited from staff such as these that we are all able to celebrate 50 years of continuous productive work and to look forward to the next 50 with confidence.

Mark O'Brien was born in 1945 and grew up on a sheep farm in New England, NSW, was educated by the De La Salle Brothers in Armidale, and completed a BSc at the University of New England in 1967. He joined the Dominican Order in 1967 and studied for the priesthood in Canberra and Dublin, Ireland, being ordained in Dublin in 1973. He completed a License in Sacred Scripture (LSS) at the Biblicum in Rome in 1976 and commenced lecturing in Old Testament/Hebrew Bible studies at YTU in 1977. He undertook doctoral studies part-time at the then Melbourne College of Divinity (MCD) with Tony Campbell SJ as his supervisor, and completed the degree in 1987. He was Academic Dean of YTU from 1990 to 1993 when he was elected Provincial of the Dominican Friars in Australia, NZ, PNG and the Solomon Islands. After two terms as Provincial, he taught Old Testament for over three years in the Catholic Institute of Sydney (CIS). Upon his return to Melbourne, he was delighted to be able to resume teaching OT at YTU and at CTC and continued to do so until his retirement at the end of 2021.

YTU in Revue

CHRIS CHAPLIN MSC

I was a student at Yarra Theological Union in the 1980s. For me, the main purpose of being there was to complete studies required for ordination. I am now somewhat embarrassed to acknowledge that while the studies held little interest for me personally at the time, in subsequent years I see with gratitude the foundations they provided. At the time, I was inspired by many women and some men who undertook studies at YTU purely out of personal and pastoral interest. These individuals and those belonging to the member religious congregations were in those days a close-knit community. Many of them had friendships and mutual social connections beyond the classroom, and while not a natural extrovert I enjoyed the company of many of them.

A tradition of the Yarra Theological Union meant that founding religious congregations had a representative on the

Student Representative Council. In due time, I too served my time in this role. I recall that the engagement of students in extracurricular activities was a highlight. Yes, there were the normal student concerns to be taken to administration, such as coffee being available in the recreation room, the occasional representative act on behalf of students, or forming a choir to sing at graduation time. But one of the most memorable involvements I had was the annual YTU Revue. These were moments of extraordinary creativity, connection, and comedy. Not only for students but also for staff, families of lay-students and staff, and seminarians from the member congregations.

Mandatory at the annual Revue were performances by each of the member congregation; Franciscans, Passionists, O.Carms, Dominicans, Redemptorists, SVD's, Pallotines, and MSC. Their antics were generally hilarious, and at times a little risqué, but always in good humour and within the boundaries of decency. Humour was accompanied by song, poetry, and musicianship. Dominicans including Mark O'Brien, in flowing white robes presenting their translation of 'Psalm 23', or Adrian Hellwig's memorable 'Phonetic Punctuation', Franciscans singing 'Pigeon Ponds' and 'Establishment Blues', the SVDs in rubber boots and shorts on mission in the Garden of Eden, or their 'excerpt from the Don Lane Show', 'the Yarra Boy's Lament', a Rock Musical called 'Graffita', and even the SRC elections were not quarantined from satire's barb. But sweet revenge came in 1981 when the SRC cat-walked its version of 'Faculty Fashions'.

We witnessed that the several women and married students could easily equal anything that the seminarians could dish up – a duet of 'Noel and Gertrude' for example – only to be matched by 'Anthony and Cleopatra' by the YTU President and Dean. The staff too were not left wanting, as many of them took to the stage, either to recite prose or poetry, or to lampoon themselves, each other, or the system. No one will ever forget Tony Kelly's recital of (insert here any variety of wine) Nowotny!! Not too many sacred cows escaped the performer's wit. Even the themes of those Revues were creative, giving me (on most Revue committees) licence to create some elaborate stage scenery. The 1980 Revue was 'Play it Again, Y.T.U' – As Time Goes By'. 1981 was threateningly called 'Yes folks, it's that time of the year again ...'. The most creative was perhaps the doctrinally correct, 'Extra YTU Nulla Salus' and the memorable 'YTU Back to the Future'. The Revue was always a combination of fun with food. SRC appointed a Revue committee who determined if it be catered or bring to share. Favourites included born-again chicken, cold meat a la Gnosticism, salad so healthy you could leap Joan Nowotny's desk, rice so white and fluffy you would think you were at lectures, all topped off with a tasty dolce that was more liberating than Segundo!

YTU studies had their place. But when we come together from those days, these are the stories we tell. And we laugh. And we remember with gratitude.

Chris Chaplin, Missionary of the Sacred Heart, student at YTU, 1980-1986. He took vows in 1984, ordained in 1988. After 6 years in a Darwin parish, he completed the SILOAM Certificate in Spiritual Direction from Heart of Life, Melbourne. He went on to facilitate retreats for staff and students of Australian MSC Colleges. In 1997, he began three years of eremitical life. He worked in initial formation in the Pacific Islands for 6 years, was a member of the MSC Pacific Council, and had two years as Principal of Chevalier Farm Training Centre, Fiji. Upon returning to Australia, he served 3 years as Director of St Mary's Towers Retreat Centre, Douglas Park, before resuming eremitical life for a further 9 years. His ministry as a psychotherapist/facilitator has been the mainstay of his life, He currently serves as a member of the MSC General Leadership Team, Rome, with the ongoing formation portfolio and the geographical mandate of Asia-Australia.

Creative Initiative at YTU

KATHLEEN WILLIAMS RSM

In the nine years during which I had some responsibility for YTU, four as Academic Dean, then five as President, I was impressed by the extent to which members of the College – students, past students, staff and faculty – exercised initiative, sometimes with quite amazing creativity. There are too many people to name, so I'm hoping that as I recall some relevant events people will recognise themselves and others, and that remembering will give them the joy it has given me.

A newsletter was set up and named 'A Little Yeast', the very name inviting articles that recognised the way in which theology can not only transform people but also enable them to reach potential that otherwise might have remained unrealised.

Two women, having suffered along with all the other students on those hard chairs that had been at YTU from the beginning, raised the money – the full cost – to replace them with the much more comfortable and very much better-looking ones now in use.

The Australian Bishops conducted a survey they entitled 'Why Catholics don't go to Mass'. When we decided to have an evening that was a theological and sociological response to it at YTU, one woman said 'Let's call it *Missing from the Table*'. What a felicitous change of focus: from data to relationship! The person responsible for the Bishop's survey noted: 'I wish we had thought of that'.

Two celebrations of International Women's Day were organised. At the first one, a dinner, a New Zealand woman was the guest speaker and she spoke of the death of her mentally challenged son and of the garden planted at the place where he had fallen to his death, established partly in his honour and partly to have a place where other residents could find peace. The response to her very moving account was twofold: a theological reflection and a dance. The second celebration featured the Young Australian of the Year – a young Aboriginal woman – as guest speaker.

Two art exhibitions were curated by the then YTU Promotions person. Some fine pieces were shown, and there was conversation about the age-old link between religion and art, a link on which theology draws.

There was a Medieval Debate evening – with appropriate dress; an Italian night – with all things Italian.

The conversion of the building housing the former Franciscan Printing Press and Bindery to what was to be the Graduate Study Centre – at no cost to the Franciscans – called for many creative initiatives to raise the required funds. Attractive events were organised. One ex-student donated the full cost of carpeting the area, $10,000, with just one request: that the carpet be good quality wool. Others organised events behind the scenes to raise money they could then donate. When the Study Centre was being planned, the architect (whose services were all pro bono) was asked to come up with a design that would be functional for its intended purpose but also able to be readily adapted by the Franciscans if the time came when YTU no longer needed the building. The request set his creative juices flowing, with an impressive result.

The creative contributions to the SRC evenings were many and diverse, sometimes very entertaining. Amongst them, who would ever forget the very young family who acted out Pope Francis ' *Laudato Si'*, demonstrating remarkable understanding of its ecological and social aspects and of the link between them?

Remember the introduction of Hospitality Week? It was initiated by a woman for whom nothing symbolised welcome more than shared food. She also had a gift for organising and getting others to work with her, with the result that for a whole week two full hot meals were provided each day, one at lunch and one in the evening, to give the opportunity for new students to feel part of the college and for all students and their lecturers to get to know each other.

This is just a sample of the creativity and initiative that have so enriched YTU. No doubt many more will come to mind as we think back over these fifty years.

Kathleen Williams is an Australian Sister of Mercy, with qualifications in education, education administration, in theology (Masters and Doctorate). She lectured in systematic theology at Yarra Theological Union, her areas of focus included grace and theological anthropology, method in theology and mystical theology. She has a particular research interest is the work of Canadian Jesuit priest, philosopher and theologian Bernard Lonergan, her doctoral dissertation, Lonergan and the transforming immanence of the transcendent: towards a theology of grace as the dynamic state of being-in-love with God, 1998, MCD. She is a former member of the Executive Council of WCATI (World Conference of Associations of Theological Institutions). More recently, she has been involved in designing and implementing a program in theology for the women religious sisters in Papua New Guinea.

YTU Making Space

ROBYN REYNOLDS OLSH

When I think of YTU (Yarra Theological Union), I think first of the place, the grounds, the green grass, my very favourite gum tree, the kingfishers outside my upstairs office. I think too of the beautiful chapel with its magnificent stained-glass window. I see the monastery courtyard where Indigenous leader, Vicky (Walker) Clarke once led a simple smoking ceremony for our opening class. I see the downstairs verandahs where, despite Covid times, students and staff still sit and spend time together. Place is important. As is space.

The YTU community makes space, finds space – especially for ones who might otherwise perhaps not find a place, a home, an inclusive environment. YTU makes extra effort to find places – academically, culturally, physically, socially... to be a welcoming space. In recent years, having the connection with the Korean School of Theology and with the English Language School for Pastoral Ministry has been mutually enriching.

Over the years – and in the years since I have been at YTU – different and new roads have been taken, adaptations made, exciting initiatives taken – some have been isolated 'events', others longer term. I recall when YTU sponsored a wonderful gathering for International Women's Day. In 2009, I was a founding member of Social Policy Connections which in 2016 paved the way for passing on the baton to the University of Divinity's New Centre for Research in Religion and Social Policy. In 2019, there was real pride in witnessing YTU leadership in sponsoring and co-delivering the outstanding Voices of Hope and Challenge Conference.

Perhaps a recent engagement might best capture YTU's essence for me: A colleague and I, each of us carrying a bag of books, took a short walk through our lovely grounds to the UD's new School of Indigenous Studies. Naomi Wolfe, First People's Coordinator – knowing I had some books to pass on - had suggested a midday meeting. Naomi responded positively and generously to an invitation by my colleague – to meet with her class in first semester. So, YTU through the years: respectful engaging with all (especially, surely, with our First Peoples), and making spaces for genuine conversations, for significant learning and teaching and for life-giving, life-growing experiences. When the heart is open, the Spirit breathes!

> *Robyn Reynolds, OLSH Sister, spent many years working with Aboriginal people in the Northern Territory, in Nungalinya College, Darwin. She is on the Faculty at YTU and lectures at the Heart of Life Centre, Malvern.*

Those Who Serve Spirit and Light

MATTHEW BECKMAN OFM

And we should honour and respect all who do theology and those who minister the most holy Divine Words as those whose who serve spirit and life to us!
St Francis of Assisi, *Testament*

I spent a little time pondering the question that I had been set for this piece: 'someone/something in your experience at YTU that was important to you'. My first thoughts flew to the distinctive and 'larger than life' (and larger than two lives in some cases!) teachers that stand out so vividly in the memory of my own time at YTU. Those characters like Angelo O'Hagan, Joan Nowotny, Tony Kelly and John McCristal are sure to feature prominently on other pages within this volume.

Yet, as I reflected further, I conceded that while these were towering figures in my recollections and a fruitful source of anecdotes by the score, the truth is that they were not the experiences that were most important to me. That laurel falls on the brow of the students of YTU. Many are only names now and little known but they shaped my life, and its direction, more than any teacher I ever had.

I include in that body of students those with whom I studied and who kept me amused when boring lectures failed to accomplish that. These were the ones with whom I talked, argued, and discussed, as we tried to fit what we had heard in class into the context of a world that was rapidly changing around us, perhaps faster than our teachers realised. When too much abstraction and philosophical speculation took my focus upward a little too stratospherically, these students were the friends who kept me grounded and ensured that I stayed healthily grounded.

Even more, I include among that body of students the ones that now currently I teach, for eventually I made my way back to YTU. Better than my peers of the earlier generation, they excel at an honesty and a challenge to provide them with the tools and knowledge that is apt for a ministry and for a world for which I myself had not been trained. They will move in a quite different church and world than the one around us now. They are experts at keeping my eyes looking forward to the horizon with expectation and confidence, rather than the fear that can assail too many in our church. These are the people who inspire me; to embark on the journey of theological education is a courageous step in a world that both dismisses yet hungers for what these students will offer.

Their enthusiasm, energy, dedication and understanding afford me a satisfaction that is the unique reward of teachers.

Their passion and their questions have, I know, saved me from jadedness and indifference on occasions – not to mention quite a few mistakes! It is hard to feel old and pessimistic at YTU. So, to the 'someones' who were important to me at YTU – to Anna, Sean, Adam, Helene from years long past, and to Toub, Maria, Kris and Heather and all the many others of more recent years – my thanks for being such a rich and significant part of my experience of YTU and for making me who I am.

> *Matthew Beckmann is a Franciscan friar who teaches in the areas of Systematic Theology and Church History. His interests lie in the interplay of those two disciplines, how historical events shape theology and how theology, in turn, drive history. He is a medievalist by training but also works with the theological ideas about salvation and redemption, the theology and history of the Franciscan Order and how theological ideas are disseminated and diffused. He has worked for many years in the area of Justice, Peace and the Integrity of Creation and is part of the University's Centre for Religion and Social Policy. He enjoys being back at YTU where he began his theological studies.*

My Experience of Yarra Theological Union

ROSIE JOYCE CSB

I started lecturing at YTU in February 1996 and every Monday afternoon I travelled from Ballarat for the evening lecture. Invariably I would meet John Hill and we would have our weekly discussions over a cup of tea and TimTam biscuits – I know that I ate many more than him!

After a couple of weeks, Laurie Nemer invited me to join him for a meal, the aim being to get to know each other better. It was the beginning of a pattern of support which I quickly found out was a hallmark of YTU and led me to deeply appreciate the community of which I was now a part.

Yarra Theological Union is Catholic in tradition and ecumenical in spirit and we are enriched by having faculty and students from different faith traditions. These different understandings of the mystical add richness to our communal search for the truth and the sacred amid the messiness of life. The freedom of thought and the expression of one's truth is life-giving and adds honesty in the search for the Divine.

Many of the students come from different parts of the world and they bring with them a diversity of thought and life experiences. Our world becomes larger and more diverse and our certainties become less certain! We have much to be grateful for the perspectives on life which they bring along with the richness of many cultures.

I finished lecturing at YTU at the end of 2000 in order to take on a position of leadership in my congregation. How delighted I was when, having concluded that ministry, I was again invited back to lecture at YTU at the beginning of 2009! I find in YTU a spiritual home where I am nourished and challenged to do my part to make the world and our church a better place. In turn, I am enriched with a sense of hope in the future.

> *Rosie Joyce is a Brigidine Sister whose early ministry was in secondary school teaching and leadership. Since gaining her licentiate in canon law, Rosie has worked in the Marriage Tribunal where she is currently a judge for Victoria and Tasmania. During her time in congregational leadership, she was President of Catholic Religious Australia. Rosie lectures in canon law at YTU and is a canonical consultant for many religious congregations.*

The Changing Shape of Christian Ministry

JOHN N. COLLINS

1997 marked the beginning of my professional connection with YTU as a visiting lecturer in the Department of Christian Thought and History. My course was *The Changing Shape of Christian Ministry c. 50-400 CE*.

In the previous year, I had resigned from my responsibilities as Religious Education Co-ordinator at John Paul College in Frankston to move into part-time teaching of Biblical Studies at Loreto Mandeville Hall. My hopes were of freer time for writing. Just then, however, I received an invitation from Fr Tony Kelly to teach a course on ministry at YTU. This was an exciting intervention.

What prompted it, I presume, were impressions he took of my 1992 paperback *Are All Christians Ministers?* His reviewer's blurb called the book 'a resource no one can afford to ignore'.

The book was, of course, a spin-off from my research volume of 1990, itself a revamp of my 1976 thesis at the

University of London King's College, *Diakonia: Re-interpreting the Ancient Sources*.

This study aimed to turn the scales on how we were to evaluate the function of ministry in the early church, and to take whatever leads we might discern from there to our considerations of the church we lived in. The whole exercise arose from the values attaching to the New Testament Greek term *diakonia* that I had identified in my work of re-interpretation during the years 1971-75.

A delicate topic: a mandated activity for some within the community? or a call upon all from their baptism?

By 2005, Benedict XVI would seem to have closed that conversation in stating in his first encyclical *God is love* (n. 21): '*diakonia* – the ministry of charity exercised in a communitarian, orderly way – became part of the fundamental structure of the church'.

And his successor regularly reinforces the 'service' element in reminding even 'the greatest among you' to be 'the one who serves, always in service' (25 October 2013).

This call arises, of course, from 'the God who came not to be served but to serve' (the *diakon-* term at Matthew 20:28/Mark 10:45), as Pope Francis emphasised in his Christmas address to the Roman Curia in 2017. So profound is 'this ministerial, petrine and curial finality of service' that Francis invoked the phrase '*diaconal primacy*' to establish the defining character of ecclesial activities.

Novel in papal teachings, 'diaconal primacy' had begun establishing itself as a working principle within German Evangelical Churches since the 1830s. By the 1930s, the second volume of Kittel's authoritative *Theological Dictionary of the*

New Testament devoted 13 pages (German ed. 1935; Eng. trans. 1964) to elaborating a semantic profile of the Greek *diakon-* words, this culminating in phrases about 'loving assistance rendered to the neighbour... understood as full and perfect sacrifice... the very essence of service'. The German churches' national welfare department, with almost 600,000 employees today, carries the simple German title *Diakonie* (see *diakonie.de*, English page).

Meantime, in 2000, Frederick Danker introduced the re-interpretation into the 3rd edition of the classic Bauer, Arndt, Gingrich *Greek-English Lexicon of the New Testament*. This initiative was endorsed in 2007 by Dr Anni Hentschel of Wurzburg in her semantic study, *Diakonia im Neuen Testament*.

Henceforward, theology would have to reckon with the fact that the Greek *diakon-* terms never once expressed notions of service as benevolent.

Reporting this, however, I also record that my most recent purchase was *International Handbook of Ecumenical Diakonia* (published August, 2021): over 700 octavo pages of 104 contributions extolling 'best practices in Christian social service'. On order: *The Diaconal Church* (August, 2019).

As emeritus of YTU in 2012, I noticed the course replacing mine: 'as one who serves'...

> *John Neil Collins studied Scripture in Rome, taught at Daramalan College, Canberra, and John Paul II College, Frankston. During this time, he researched and wrote on Diakonia, publishing internationally and ecumenically.*

Te Deum

Cecilia Francisco-Tan

Te Deum
Not because of victories
I sing,
having none,
but for the common sunshine,
the breeze,
the largesse of the spring.

Not for victory
but for the day's work done
as well as I was able;
not for a seat upon the dais
but at the common table.[1]

Charles Reznikoff 1894-1976

---

[1] Reznikoff Charles, https://poets.org/poem/te-deum accessed 21 April 2022.

Charles Reznikoff's poem captures the essence and spirit of YTU since its inception 50 years ago. Let me sing praises for the 'common sunshine, the breeze, the largesse of spring' of God's Spirit hovering over this place, drawing us towards God's 'common table', within the particularity of our lives. It is here, *all* are 'conceived and born and reared'[2] in a continual cycle, of discovering and deciding what all are to make of themselves as persons. The calm and beautiful surrounds is balm. The greatest fruits result in the shared encounters against this appropriate background. Let me share some of these fruits.

I returned as a faculty member in January 2022, after fifteen years as a student of YTU with a brief hiatus in-between. 'Homecoming,' comes to mind together with a genuine knowledge that here I will be valued for who I am, for my contribution, without self-censorship, compromise, fear or favour, largely because of the YTU experience.

YTU is more than a theological college to attain formal accreditation. Theological education *as a human good*, to meet the cultural, social, ecclesiological and theological needs post Vatican II, is fundamental to the YTU enterprise. The spirit of freedom to critique, to decide, and act on what is 'good' is perhaps YTU's greatest asset and source of success. Good theological education, to bring out the best innate human qualities in the desire to know God, occurs through maturing optimal intellectual and spiritual development in *all* members at YTU. Unifying the many truths meaningfully and

---

[2] Lonergan Bernard, *Method in Theology* (Toronto: University of Toronto Press, 1971), 79.

collaboratively in the concrete, believing that as God's people, progress and transformation are possible, even when it is not obvious, makes YTU a place and source of hope.

The culture involving collaborators, friends, learners, all seekers of truth at YTU, has evolved. I offer one perspective. Suffice to say, many have been instrumental to my own being and becoming. Many are now life-long friends across many cultures, languages, in Australia and overseas. These are the true gifts to be cherished.

I mention those significant to me. Kathleen Williams RSM, my PhD Supervisor, mentor, and friend lives 'friendly conversation'. Our continued dialogue expands my own insights into the value and work of Bernard Lonergan SJ. Priceless gifts are so, because of the giver and Kathleen's tremendous charity, support, and encouragement in my deepest and darkest of times cannot be overstated. Her latest comment to me: There is always 'Love to spare and share' is worthwhile remembering as YTU moves into the next fifty years and beyond. The late Peter Price, my co-supervisor, through his own life and death, is the epitome of the 'good and faithful servant', who lived fully the baptismal call to be priest, prophet and royal. He is a reminder of the why, the how and what of theological education. He claimed his birth-right as God's beloved. Dare we do the same?

Bernard Teo CSsR and I form the Singaporean 'diaspora' at YTU. Over three years (2014-2016), we organised Spirituality days for Melburnians of South-East Asian heritage at the Redemptorist monastery, Kew. Seizing the moment to meet needs when they arise is another fruit. Bernard, together with the late Cormac Nagle OFM formed the dynamic duo in

Moral Theology. They personified the collaborative friendship necessary for good theology.

Bruce Duncan CSsR opened my eyes to the richness and sometimes short-sightedness of the social encyclicals, and the Australian Catholic Church. Bruce, in his understated way, communicated the importance of *ressourcement* – of returning to the sources for truth and therefore rejuvenation – a critical task for all involved in theological praxis.

To this day, I attribute my research skills, and historical criticism to Will Johnston, Peter Price and the late Larry Nemer SVD. Larry continued to correspond with me three weeks prior to his passing. This small story of 'three white men and one Asian woman' demonstrates how the intersections of history, culture, race, and gender need not be barriers to finding a place at the common table – an important insight for the increasingly multicultural makeup at YTU.

How appropriate that my sacramental theology professor, Brian Gleeson, CP, and I continue to share a deep friendship over shared meals, and recipes! Brian, to this day, reveals a pastor's heart to both my husband and me, as we navigate through the different seasons of our lives. In partaking of one another's lives, the source and summit of the spirituality proclaimed at YTU is a profound gift available to all. There are many others, too many to name, and each offers precious nuggets of why good theological education matters. These good people, with their variety of gifts coming from the same Spirit, walk the holy ground at YTU, leaving imprints on many hearts. They have done so for fifty years, believing in theological education as a human good. With faith, hope and charity, may this value continue to hold as YTU evolves.

Cecilia Francisco-Tan has a PhD and is the 2020 recipient of the University of Divinity's Vice-chancellor's student award for YTU and the 2020 Lonergan Institute Post-Doctoral Fellowship Award, Boston College. She is current editor of the Australian Lonergan Workshop and represents YTU on the University of Divinity's Education Board.

YTU, A Community Seeking God

CATHERINE MCCAHILL SGS

A vibrant, learning, searching community is my lasting memory of Yarra Theological Union.

The students came from many and diverse backgrounds: older women and men exploring new understandings of God in their 'retirement'; mature, hardworking persons undertaking tertiary study for the first time with all the attendant excitement and anxiety of such; professional people studying to enhance their ministry with enthusiasm to go deeper and make this more than an academic exercise and some with the reluctance that comes from the necessity of contracts and expectations; young women and men new to religious life eager to learn but sometimes burdened by the complexities of language, culture and requirements; and young men embarked on the path to ordination. This was our classroom and 'indeed it was very good'.

Often, I found myself pondering and appreciating the richness of the experience. Diversity of culture, Christian tradition, religious charism, life experience and work situations all contributed to the exploration of God and the things of God – creation, humanity, church and so much more. There was freedom to ask questions, to explore ideas and seek the One who is Truth. Each person was a valued contributor in the communal endeavour. Religious life and ordination were valued but not privileged. I doubt that any theologate could surpass this benchmark in the formation of priestly candidates.

The classroom experience always flowed beyond into expressions of community in the common room, in liturgies, in the library, and into special occasions of celebration. Mostly, we experienced support and encouragement from each other, opportunities to share the more of life.

Supporting this vibrant classroom community, I encountered a wise and passionate community of staff, all committed to a common purpose. Drawn from the founding male religious congregations, female religious congregations, and the wider Christian church, from Australia and various other countries, these women and men became a theologising community. Research, resources, stories and life were shared for the good of all. Non-teaching staff – administration and library – were a vital part of the venture.

There were challenges as in any Christian community. My own part of this story coincided with the 2008 Review of Australian Higher Education, the emergence of TEQSA (Tertiary Education Quality and Standards Agency) and the application by the Melbourne College of Divinity to become a Specialist University. Much was required of staff, especially the lecturers by these new realities. My abiding sense is of the collaboration and cooperation for the greater good. Re-writing course outlines and assessments in the new compliance regime was a challenge. Audits provided a different type of challenge. Throughout all of this, I experienced the generosity and commitment of the community in a new way.

Collaboration with the other Colleges of the University of Divinity strengthened and I am sure, continues to strengthen the community of YTU. The classroom presence of students from other Colleges and opportunities for team teaching with faculty from those Colleges expanded our thinking and theologising.

Finally, I give thanks for all that was and is YTU. In that classroom and in that staffroom, I was blessed, enriched, challenged, and supported to become a better teacher, to become a more authentic human being, to continue my own journey of seeking God.

> *Catherine McCahill began life in North Queensland. Since joining the Sisters of the Good Samaritan her main ministry has been in education – secondary and tertiary. Her theological studies were undertaken within the Melbourne College of Divinity (now University of Divinity) with research in the Second Testament and Christian Religious Education. She was the Academic Dean at YTU from 2008-2012. Currently, she is on the leadership team of the Sisters of the Good Samaritan.*

Art Enhances Theological Education

CLAIRE RENKIN

I began teaching at YTU in February 2001. With my husband Will, who later taught the survey of church history at YTU, I had returned to Melbourne after a number of years living in Massachusetts. Our move back to my home city was a leap of faith – academic jobs here were scarce, and I had no idea of what the future held for me. During a chance meeting with Maryanne Confoy, a former teacher of mine, she urged me to meet with the then president of YTU, Paul Chandler. Over coffee, we discussed my conviction that the rich artistic heritage of Christian art offered a different lens through which everyone can encounter the sacred in Christian life and theology. By supplying a language distinct from texts, visual art evokes theological experience with a rare directness. Visual experience offers the same sort of glimpses of the divine that moments in nature or hearing a musical performance sometimes deliver us.

Back in 2000, I had no idea how I was going to develop these aspirations into units that contributed to students studying theological disciplines. However, I benefitted hugely from the support and commitment of colleagues like Paul, Joan Nowotny and Kathleen Williams, who shared my passion for exploring how art can enhance theological education. The encouragement and openness of colleagues and students at YTU inspired my teaching and research. At YTU, for the first time in my career, I discovered a community of learning where studying theology opens up all that it means to feel at home in the household of God. My life has been immensely enriched by friendships with everyone in the YTU community.

No other space at YTU captures so well the essence of a place as the cloister, where all – including the guinea pigs – are received with respect and kindness. Designed and built by the Franciscan friars some eighty years ago, this grassy, tree-filled space bounded by arcades on four sides perpetuates a key feature of Christian monastic and mendicant life. Built at the physical heart of YTU, the cloister evokes an ancient wisdom that carries forward the teachings of the desert mothers and fathers: this place provides hospitality to all who seek the way of the Lord. Indeed, at times the cloister can seem to embody the promise of Eden as the garden where life-giving water always quenches the seeker's thirst. Similarly, for decades, wisdom figures at YTU like Campion Murray and Larry Nemer personified for me and for many others a commitment to the sharing of conversation. I must confess that among all the cancellations of events at YTU that Covid restrictions imposed, the most painful was the cancellation of Hospitality Week at the beginning of the new academic year! I look forward to resuming this tradition in our 51st Year!!

Claire Renkin has been teaching art history and spirituality at YTU since 2001. Her teaching areas include the art and architecture of the Early Christians and Byzantium, and the art and spirituality of the late Middle Ages. In addition to these topics, Claire co-teaches units on death, dying and bereavement in art and spirituality, and the history of Mary in the Christian tradition. In addition to her teaching at YTU, she lectures regularly throughout Australia on the intersection of visual art, theology and spirituality. Her research and publications focuses on the role of gender and devotion in depictions of female sanctity in European art from the late Middle Ages to the early modern period, c. 1350-1650. Claire, together with Sr Angela Slattery IBVM, is researching a little-known cycle of fifty paintings of the life of Mary Ward 1585-1645, the founder of the Institute of the Virgin Mary also known as Loretos.

Dean of YTU

ROSS FISHBURN

I came to YTU in 2011 as Associate Dean, after 13 years working at Trinity College as Director of Studies at the Theological School, and teaching at the United Faculty of Theology. It was quite a change of culture for me to acquire a new family. My wife calls my 'loud Irish family' where the faculty room is a focus of fellowship and what I call the 'hilarity of the saints'. The welcome given to this stray Anglican was warm from the outset and has remained so for the next 11 years. In 2012, I succeeded Catherine McCahill SGS as Academic Dean, and I've been teaching a few units in Systematic Theology throughout my time here.

These years have been years of change for YTU. 2012 saw the Melbourne College of Divinity become a University. This has brought not merely a change of name but something of a change of style to our work. Our accountability is now not simply to MCD centrally, but more broadly to the government through the Tertiary Education Quality and Standards Agency (as it is now called). We must ensure that the university's policy framework is compliant with the Higher Education Standards Framework set by the government. The compliance pressure feels more constant than the former pattern of being audited every 5 years.

We've also seen significant staffing changes. We've farewelled Peter Price and Glenda Bourke both of whom died too soon after their retirement. Larry Nemer retired early in my time here, and sadly died last year. Emeritus Professor Christiaan Mostert came to us very much in the manner of Norman Young, after concluding his ministry at the Uniting Church College. He retired from YTU in 2020. Kathleen Williams, Bruce Duncan, John Hill, Mark O'Brien, have all retired from teaching in the last few years. We've welcomed Gavin Brown, Janina Heibel, Anne Gardner, Matthew Beckmann, Carmel Posa, Barry Rogers, Cecilia Tan, Donna Neanderand Audrey Statham. They have all been welcome additions to the teaching faculty. In 2021, we welcomed Professor John McDowell as Associate Dean. He brings significant experience to our leadership team both from within this University and from the Universities of Newcastle (NSW) and Edinburgh. This year, we were very sad to lose Janette Elliott (Bredenoord) after 12 years as Registrar, but have recently welcomed Adam Couchman to succeed her.

The student body has changed as well. We are blessed to still have an active core of seminarians from our religious orders. Not only do they provide a stable core to our communal life, but they enrich it by the diversity of cultures they embody. We have fewer students doing theology for interest or professional development than we once did, but this is still an important part of our ministry. Perhaps the biggest change is the decline in the B.Theol. While this is still an important degree program for seminarians, our 'lay' students now tend to enrol in the shorter postgraduate programs as more fitting to their needs.

One thing remains the same: the ethos of YTU as a place of welcome and inclusion, catholic in tradition and ecumenical in spirit. This ethos is firmly in place and has been in evidence throughout my time here. *Ad multos annos!*

> *Ross Fishburn has been involved in theological education and ministry formation since 1994. His academic interests are in ecclesiology, ecumenical studies and the history and theology of the Anglican Church, and he has taught in these and other areas of Christian Thought and History. He currently teaches the units CT1/8003Y Beginning With Jesus, and CT2/3/9016Y In Search of a Humbler Church. From 1998-2010, he was Director of Studies in the Theological School at Trinity College, Melbourne, while also teaching in the United Faculty of Theology within the MCD. He came to YTU in 2011 as Assistant Dean and became Academic Dean in April 2012. He is a priest of the Anglican Church of Australia of some 35 years standing, and currently is an honorary associate priest at St Paul's Canterbury where his wife, Rachel McDougall, is the Vicar*

YTU Reflections: Grace as a Just Hospitality

JOHN C. MCDOWELL
Associate Dean

It was in 2015 that I first visited YTU in my capacity as the University's Director of Research. The College soon came to have a special place within the fond and productive memories of my time in the Research Office. Lest that sound clichéd, it can be elaborated in a variety of ways.

The College is grounded in a love of the Christian tradition *at its best*, where that tradition particularly takes its place around what Augustine's *De Doctrina Christiana* depicts as the reading of the scriptures together for the cultivation of the love of God that overflows in love of neighbour. Such a reading performance is shaped by an engagement with, and grounding in, a living out of the scriptures' irreducible witness to the love of God for all God's creatures.

Love-talk can tend towards sentimentality. When robustly, or better, appropriately ordered, love as hospitality is exceptionally demanding of the one who loves and of the processes within which love is offered and received. It is a radical act in that it disrupts the systems conducive to the narrowing of who is to be loved – whether that be the privileging of the love of self, or the restriction of love to those who are like oneself. To love God, or rather, to continually learn to become those purified in embodying the generous Self-giving of God, is to consistently express the love of the One whose grace is fully expansive. Grace embraces and communicatively ingathers *all things* in its creative and redemptive agency. Here, the College's sensibility has been deeply informed by attending to this plenitudinous expansiveness through consequent concern for setting considerations of socio-economic, political, and ecological justice in terms of the proper flourishing of all things together.

The College reminds us that God-talk, or the way of living as the assembled witnesses to the life-givingness of God, does not come as a gift to be triumphalistically grasped and possessed, or, worse, wielded as a weapon against others. On the contrary, God's communicative presence keeps on giving. This is what provides the condition for the transfigurative life of hospitality, friendship, solidarity, and zealous resistance to the powers and authorities that distort and diminish the proper wellbeing of all things. The hospitable environment that has been cultivated at the College is uniquely configured around a communal response to this reconciled communion that the God of Jesus Christ draws the world into. Such a hospitality not only conditions the engagement with strangers (which I once was), but equally the support for, and encouragement of, students and colleagues (the latter which I was blessed to become in 2021).

The College's ecumenical ethos that attends to others' voices from within the Christian tradition generates not only a cooperativeness that is appropriate to God's reconciling embrace of everything, but also a humble accountability to the presence of the parabolic within the world. I have experienced the College's way in, and for, the world as anything but that of a *contra mundum* that denies the hope given by the redemptive divine embrace. Instead, YTU demonstrates continually its commitment to the integrity of the Gospel-life that celebrates its pattern of being in the figure of the One who kenotically continues to bear scars in his risen life. It is hardly surprising, then, that the College is deeply committed to serving the mission of God through encouraging healthy church.

The words of Pope Francis in *Evangelii Gaudium* encapsulate my experience of the College, and it is with them that I will close:

> No one can strip us of the dignity bestowed upon us by this boundless and unfailing love. With a tenderness which never disappoints, but is always capable of restoring our joy, he makes it possible for us to lift up our heads and to start anew.

John C. McDowell is Associate Dean at Yarra Theological Union, and Professor of Philosophy, Systematic Theology, and Ethics. Formerly, he was Academic Dean at St Athanasius College, the Director of Research at the University of Divinity, Morpeth Chair of Theology & Religion at the University of Newcastle NSW, the Meldrum Lecturer at the University of Edinburgh, and a student at the Universities of Cambridge and Aberdeen. He is author of 7 monographs, 9 edited collections, and over 70 peer-reviewed articles and papers.

From the Corporate World to a Theological College

Peter Whiting

I commenced my B.Theol at YTU on the eve of the new millennium. With a gap of nearly thirty years in tertiary studies and a major life change under way, I confess to being somewhat apprehensive and uncertain. Would a middle-aged escapee from the corporate world fit into a theological college? I need not have been concerned.

As I walked up from the carpark on that first day of lectures, I fell into step with someone I presumed was a fellow student. Not so! On introducing myself I learnt that I was walking and talking with Bruce Duncan, one of my lecturers to be. Now a bit short of twenty-five years later, we remain good friends and have collaborated on a range of activities centred on social justice issues, not to mention some pleasant meals and good company shared.

The good company theme became my experience of YTU I recall pleasant conversations in the common room with a range of students, some my age, others much younger, some Australian born and others from diverse countries of origin. I recall with pleasure classroom discussions which were enriched by the lived experience of both student and lecturer alike. I guess most of all, I enjoyed the relaxed way in which experience and learning were exchanged.

It was also very refreshing to have an ecumenical perspective in our dialogues. The shared experience and insight of a female student who was an Anglican priest left quite an impression on me. As a student, I found Norman Young as a lecturer, deeply versed in the material he presented and as a facilitator always as interested to draw out the views present in the classroom as he was to present his own, drawn as they were from his Uniting Church background. I certainly didn't expect on enrolling to find myself singing Wesleyan hymns!

Sadly, it seems it is not fashionable these days to undertake philosophy studies in the undergraduate theology degree. I remember pondering the cosmological argument not to mention struggling with the problem of evil. Certainly, I have appreciated the insights derived from studying the contribution to western thought from classical Hellenic thought. Perhaps these are the musings of a mind more 'mature' in age, but I still consider that today's students would also be enriched by some philosophical insights.

With my background in business, it was perhaps unavoidable that I would be 'encouraged' to contribute to the College as a member of the Finance Committee. For this I guess I can thank Kathleen Williams who had such a pleasant way of influencing you to do these things. What was in my mind – a short-term commitment in 2006 – became a valued involvement through until 2022. Over those years, I have been privy to watching YTU evolve into a professionally staffed and run organisation now comfortably at home in its place as a campus of the University of Divinity.

It is a little bit fascinating to reflect on the fact that over the twenty years plus of my involvement with YTU, its situation has always been a little precarious. Yet for all its challenges (and the recent Covid problem and its aftermath is an excellent example), YTU has been able to continuously re-invent itself and find ways to continue to deliver quality theological teaching. My theological self can find the source of this minor miracle in the working of the Holy Spirit. My corporate self recognises that many have contributed by their talent and commitment to producing this outcome.

So, a well done to all those who have made YTU what is has become over the last 50 years. Certainly, I hope that many others in the coming years will come to have the joyful and challenging experience I enjoyed.

> *Peter Whiting graduated in Commerce from Melbourne University in 1970. A long career with Shell Australia followed during which he married and has now four adult children and two grandchildren. He returned to part time tertiary studies in 1999 at YTU, eventually graduating B.Theol. and Grad Dip Theol (Sys Theol). He worked with Bruce Duncan on Social Policy Issues and Justice matters, as well as the YTU Finance Committee. He is now retired but remains active in parish life and a range of other interests.*

Faith Seeking Understanding 'in Community'

GAVIN BROWN

Few would doubt that St Anselm said it best when he defined the theological enterprise as *Fides quaerens intellectum*: faith seeking understanding. At a YTU official gathering and liturgy some years ago, one student invited to speak came close – or at least made what I consider a worthy amendment. In his address, he acknowledged that theology could indeed be described as 'faith seeking understanding'. However, his experiences at YTU suggested that it was always a faith seeking understanding 'in community'. Could there be a better way of characterising fifty years of theological education at YTU? What has this looked like from my perspective?

I have had the great privilege of sitting at both ends of the YTU classroom. Initially, I undertook theological studies at YTU over a number of years. During this time, I encountered lecturers of undoubted learning and erudition, along with fellow students whose camaraderie made even the most excruciating experiences of scriptural exegesis bearable. However, what struck me most was the evident sense of community and hospitality which both nourished and enlivened all that I was learning. Shortly after my theological studies, I became a lecturer at YTU, with my teachers transforming into colleagues and – in a bizarre twist of fate – one past fellow student becoming a student in my own class (initially a little awkward for both of us, no doubt!). Yet even as a lecturer, it has been that palpable sense of community which has remained the most rewarding and precious dimension of my continuing experiences at YTU.

Now I could stop here and this would remain a worthy tribute to YTU. But it would not necessarily distinguish YTU from any institution of higher learning. Most universities these days provide students with a range of services, associations and amenities designed to foster some sense of community or at least support. What seems to characterise a sense of community I discovered at YTU is aptly encapsulated in that amended Anselmian motto: faith seeking understanding in community. This is for two major reasons, though many more could be proffered. First, some assume that 'community' – especially one within the Roman Catholic tradition – really represents a byword for 'conformity': faith seeking understanding in conformity. However, YTU finds its place in the landscape of Australian theological education as an institution and community which has always sought to nourish a questioning faith, one not afraid to tackle the difficult and sensitive challenges which all of us face as we navigate faith, reason, magisterial teaching, socio-political realities, marginalised groups, and the counter-cultural spirit of the Gospel in a secularised world. In fact, YTU has shown that only by embracing difference and diversity can a faith seeking understanding truly create community.

Secondly, and perhaps most importantly, if faith seeking understanding takes 'in community' seriously then theological education must always be oriented to the service of community. I have always found theological study at YTU immensely stimulating as an intellectual pursuit, but I have never been in any doubt that this represents a means to an end. YTU has taught me that all I have learnt – and continue to learn and impart as a lecturer – finds its telos in the building up of the ecclesial community, the Church, as an instrument in the proclamation and inbreaking Reign of God. I marvel and rejoice in the realisation that all who have passed through YTU over the last fifty years have been challenged to do precisely this. And in doing so, they have surely embodied a 'faith seeking understanding in community'.

> *Gavin Brown's interests centre upon the history and theology of Christian worship. He completed his PhD at the University of Melbourne in 2003, focusing on the history of the Eucharist in pre-Vatican II Australian Catholic culture. He has subsequently published articles on the Eucharist, liturgy and prayer in a range of journals, both local and international. Presently, Gavin is working on his first book entitled* Christ in the Antipodes: The Eucharist in the Making of the Australian Catholic Church, 1818-1962. *In addition to his position at YTU, Gavin also teaches Religious Education at St Columba's College in Essendon.*

Extensions on Datelines

BEN HO SSS

It was mid-February and I had just gotten off a long-haul flight a few days prior, returning from my Novitiate on the other side of the world in the Northern Hemisphere. As I was trying to settle back into life in Melbourne, adjusting to the time difference, and re-acclimatising, I remember rummaging through my storage boxes looking for all my previous academic qualifications so that I could finalise my registration with YTU within 48 hours. The admission team at YTU was so patient and generous to keep my application open as long as I got all the required papers in on time. Yes, I did get the papers in, by the skin of my teeth. Little did I know that requesting for extension on datelines was going to be a common theme throughout my time at YTU, especially with essays… and the lecturers were always generous to so oblige, as long as I had a legitimate reason for the requests.

YTU was a special place for me during my days of religious formation. Vocations for most religious orders or congregations within Australia are no longer 'like the good olde days' – we do not have the large numbers knocking on our doors. So being the only person in formation within my congregation, YTU was the place where I could meet others in the same situation – and not forgetting our lay sisters and brothers as well. I had found a new bunch of kindred spirits, especially the friends I made serving on the SRC. The time we spent together in and out of class was crucial for my own sanity during my time of early formation. These days, every time I go past Victoria Street, Richmond, I still reminisce the great times our 'informal formation' team shared a meal at one of these restaurants, sharing our woes and joys of being in formation.

The quality of lecturers and staff (especially those who would rather remain in the background) has been fantastic. I have chosen not to mention names here as I do not wish to run the risk of missing anyone out. They have inspired me to look beyond my current 'comfort zone' and to seek further clarification on matters that do not sit quite well with my understanding of Catholicism and Christianity in the modern day. A lot has gone into bringing the church forward; let us not miss that opportunity to keep the momentum going.

If I have to pick one most memorable event while studying at YTU it would be the lifelong friendships that I made during my time at YTU. Most have become my contemporaries in religious (and ordained) life, and they will be the ones whom I will call upon for help and company when religious life becomes lonely... hopefully not too soon.

Being part of YTU's rich history has been an honour. As a friend said to me at my 50th birthday (not too long ago), 'welcome to the other side, you are now officially a grown-up' – I would like to congratulate YTU on reaching this milestone and welcoming you to the other side ... I hope you enjoy the nice feeling of being a grown-up.

> Ben Ho was born in Singapore and emigrated to Western Australia in his early teens, where he completed high school and initial university degrees. He first encountered the Blessed Sacrament Congregation in his home parish in Perth and was also involved at St Mary's Cathedral, Perth (through the Trinity College school choir). Ben has had a varied career prior to joining religious life – he trained at the West Australian Academy of Performing Arts and went on to dance with ballet companies around the world, notably the West Australian Ballet, Pacific Northwest Ballet, and New York City Ballet. While nursing a serious injury, Ben returned to Australia and completed an accounting degree, qualified as a CPA and worked at KPMG where he was heavily involved in rolling out the GST system when it was first introduced. Still seeking to challenge himself and wanting to return to his first love of dance, Ben decided to go on to study and qualify as a physiotherapist and specialised in aiding dancers return to their career following injury.

> *Returning to the church after a long hiatus exploring spirituality in other forms and pursuing careers, Ben decided to give Catholicism a thorough 'go at it'; it was then when he found his true vocation in religious life after getting involved as a volunteer at St Francis' Church, Melbourne. Ben joined the Blessed Sacrament Congregation in 2011 and was perpetually professed in early 2017 and was ordained to the priesthood later that same year. Ben is a fully trained Clinical Counsellor and Ministry Supervisor (member of AAOS) and has finally embarked on his doctoral studies in spirituality.*

Ballarat Religious Education Accreditation Program

JONATHAN ROWE

I should begin by acknowledging the overwhelming positive experience I had while completing my Graduate Certificate in Teaching Religious Studies Education through YTU. My Diocese of Ballarat combined with YTU to support teachers across our schools, secondary and primary. I studied in 2017-18 and can still clearly remember some of our more interesting theological debates and particularly a strong sense of community that developed.

Initially, I had concerns about delving back into theology and scripture, particularly as it had been many years and my previous experience had been a little dry. I was a Deputy Principal, the only one in my group, and determined I had a fair grasp of scripture especially as I considered myself a spiritual leader of the school. What I quickly learned was that this learning, sharing of ideas, rich conversations and reflection was invigorating and I didn't know all that much!

In our first unit, Dr Rose Marie Prosser re-introduced us to the scriptures of the Old and New Testaments and how they were interpreted within the Catholic tradition. Passages from Genesis, Exodus and the Gospels of Mark, Mathew and Luke were picked apart and took on new meaning for me. Varied perspective and opinions were discussed by classmates and a depth to my understanding evolved. We shared a common goal, irrespective of our positions at our schools, and Rose Marie was masterful at teasing out our ideas and introducing concepts or perspectives we hadn't considered.

Writing in an academic style was one of the early challenges and it took me a good six months and a few assessments to start to feel confident. A few years earlier, I had completed my Masters and used a completely different academic style. I tell myself this is the reason for my difficulty but really, I think, when you stop using something you lose the skill.

The first year focused on scripture and it provided the foundation for me to move into the second which had a practical element. Rubber on the road, curriculum development and understanding of the newly introduced 'New Awakenings'. We also explored Christian choices in life, sacraments and how do we as teachers make Religion engaging for our students? It was clear, you can't do this without knowledge of scripture, the history behind the stories, the interpretation or the message and crucially a passion for this subject. Fr Philip Malone, MSC, gently guided us through. Our conversations regularly took a tangent and needed to be brought back but what great conversations they were.

At the back of the room quietly going about her work with one ear open, Gina Bernisconi, charged with organising REAP (Religious Education Accreditation Program) in the Ballarat Diocese, would regularly interject with her wisdom, adding context and placing it firmly in the teacher's or student's world or the school environment. It often felt like we had another lecturer in the room, but it also felt like she was a mother taking particularly good care of us. We were blessed.

I'm a better leader, a better teacher and have a greater connection and love for Catholic teaching, the role of Catholic schools in educating our young people and the importance of God in our lives. The REAP course opened my thoughts and eyes to many possibilities. I am convinced I am a better person for it.

> *Jonathan Rowe commenced as Principal of Monivae College in 2020. Prior to this appointment, Jonathan was Deputy Principal at Monivae College for six years. Before joining Monivae College, he was the Design Head of Department at Salesian College, Chadstone, for six years. Jonathan has a Master of Education – Wellbeing from the University of Melbourne. He has also previously held leadership positions in Design, Technology and Arts-related learning areas. Jonathan attests to having a strong faith, an authentic commitment to Catholic education and a sound knowledge of Catholic beliefs, traditions and sacramental rites. Jonathan is a strong practitioner in his own right.*

YTU and Heart of Life

BRIAN GALLAGHER MSC

YTU has permeated my years of ministry in ways that I would never have anticipated. I began as a lecturer and ended as a student!

I moved to the seminary of the Missionaries of the Sacred Heart in Croydon in 1980 as director of students. I cannot recall whether it was in that year or the following year that I found myself lecturing at YTU on 'Prayer in Christian Spirituality', a subject I had previously taught at St Paul's late vocation seminary. I lectured at YTU – and enjoyed it – for a few years.

In the process, I met other staff and the then-president Tony Kelly CSsR. Knowing my background and my interests, Tony asked me to investigate the feasibility of setting up a spirituality centre at YTU. To the disappointment of both Tony and myself, the positive plan that I presented was rejected by YTU faculty on the grounds that it was not sufficiently academic. But by coincidence, at the same time, Provincial Frank Quirk had asked me to finish in my formation ministry at Croydon. (That is another story!) So I suggested to Frank that we MSC establish the spirituality centre. Thereafter, Frank always said that he had founded Heart of Life Centre – in an indirect way, thanks to YTU. This was in 1983.

Heart of Life coloured my ministry for the rest of my life. As director, staff member, teacher, spiritual director, supervisor, encourager, I have been involved for most of Heart of Life's 40 years. I had already started a program for the formation of spiritual directors, *Siloam* (1979). That program became central to Heart of Life's several offerings. As is well documented, Heart of Life has prepared women and men from around Australia and internationally for ministry in spirituality and religious formation for all of those forty years. And still counting.

The YTU connection was not lost. I planned a Diploma of Studies in Spirituality, involving some study at YTU and attendance at a number of seminars at Heart of Life, with a major assignment at the conclusion of the 12-month program. That, too, continued for several years – until, more importantly, YTU agreed to accredit Heart of Life's program in spiritual direction. Initially, the accreditation was minimal, but later eligible students are now granted a Master's degree in Spiritual Direction, accredited at both YTU and the University of Divinity. Around the same time, Heart of Life's part-time program called Spiritual Leaders was also given credit towards a degree at YTU.

The accreditation by YTU required considerable negotiation, as academic people slowly came to accept that experiential learning was no less valuable than academic learning. Traditionally, spirituality is taught experientially – precisely because spirituality is concerned with the *experience of God*. All good spiritual writing is based on personal experience. For example, in her autobiography, Teresa of Avila wrote 'sisters, this is how God has been working in me'. At Heart of Life, we listen to personal experience, our own and our students' in a contemplative way: our teaching builds on this.

And then the turning point: after I 'retired' from Heart of Life, I decided to take up some study. One visit to YTU to look at possibilities had me enrolled as a graduate student for PhD. I became a student! I wrote a thesis entitled 'Discernment of Spirits: the Corner-stone of Formation of Spiritual Directors' based on my many years' experience in spiritual direction. The YTU support through the Director of Graduate Study, Michael Kelly, supervisors, initially Peter Price, and research seminars was crucial. The degree was granted by the University of Divinity in 2018. Three cheers for YTU.

> *Brian Gallagher, MSC, established the Heart of Life Centre which has had affiliation with YTU for many years. He lectured at YTU and also wrote a PhD thesis on Spiritual Direction and Discernment of Spirits.*

YTU 50 Years: Sharing Classrooms, Communication and Culture

PHILIP MALONE MSC

During my time teaching at St Paul's National Seminary in Sydney (1986-1998), while some of our students came with English as their second language, they were a minority and were in formation for the local Churches. This meant that our classroom concern for those students whose first language was not English was to help them 'follow' the lectures and complete their assessment tasks (including the recommended required reading entailed) in English.

But as few of us had training or skills in this, it was no mean feat – for students and staff alike.

No doubt, others will recount and rightly laud the development and success of the ELSPM program (English Language Studies Centre for Pastoral Ministry) from its visionary inception to establishment at YTU and its significant role in blending language and culture for students learning English in preparation for pastoral ministry.

I would like simply to recount here the (wonderfully positive) impact for me of working with students from other countries and cultures at YTU.

Arriving at YTU from St Paul's Seminary for first semester of 1999, I found two important differences in relation to working with students who had English as a second (or even third or fourth) language.

First, there were many more such students in our classes (sometimes exclusively so); secondly, while the expectation was (as it was in Sydney) for all students to achieve a competence in English sufficient to participate in classes and manage assignments, there was a different ethos for teaching and learning, as most of these students came from overseas and were in formation for ministry in their own cultures and Churches.

This required of us as teachers, then, not only an appropriate focus on course content, but also an important emphasis on the context(s) for the teaching/learning process so as to ensure the content was properly inculturated. What Clodovis Boff called 'feet on the ground theology'.

Students at YTU didn't simply come from other cultural (social/ecclesial) experience and leave this at the door of the classroom. They were participants as members of these cultures and Churches.

This was particularly significant for me in working with students in the fields of moral theology and liturgy. No 'one size fits all' here!

In this, the students were most helpful and supportive – not just of me but of each other, since the experience of moral norms or liturgical practice for Filipinos, say, is vastly different from that of students from PNG, China, Mexico, Madagascar, Ghana, and the vast array of countries and cultures our students came from.

It was this necessity to ensure a blend of content with context, of 'theory' with practice, that was stimulating and challenging. It was the need to work through issues to find their meaning and relevance in each cultural and ecclesial experience that energised the classes.

And it was the discussions, debates, presentations (to the class or written), the selection of assessment tasks and readings for the students relevant to their ministerial and cultural expectations, the engagement with assignments (often chosen by the students themselves as individual or group tasks), and the quality of what was presented that made teaching in this way so satisfying – and hopefully effective.

The contribution of YTU over 50 years to the local and universal Church will rightly be recognised and acknowledged.

From my perspective as one of the YTU community for some of that time, I am just grateful to have shared in this enterprise in a way that I had not expected but which has offered me the opportunity to grow as a teacher and as a person.

Philip Malone MSC has worked in the field of education, High School (teaching and administration) over eighteen years, followed by thirty five years in adult education (again, teaching and administration).

He has worked in four of the five Colleges administered by the MSC Congregation in mainland Australia, teaching RE, Indonesian, Asian Social Studies, English and History. Professional qualifications for this are BA(AS) Arts/Asian Studies, DipEd and MACE. He held senior administrative roles in three of the four Colleges.

He studied in Rome at the Academia Alfonsiana, specialising in Moral Theology, graduating STL (with a thesis exploring Euthanasia and Moral Methodology), returning to teach at St Paul's National Seminary (Kensington, Sydney) from 1987-1998, Yarra Theological Union (1999-2021), and Heart of Life Spirituality Centre (1999-2017). The primary focus here has been formation for ministry (ordained and lay) and the teaching of moral theology, liturgy, Church and Sacramental Theology, with emphasis not simply on learning but on the integration of this in experience.

He has also been a member of a number of Medical Ethics and Professional Committees.

Space to Be, Time to Ponder

EVA DABASY

After a successful but busy career, I suddenly had space when I retired – space to be and time to ponder life and where my future would lie. I suddenly had the time to address the really important questions people ask throughout their lives and to give that process the time required to enter it more deeply.

I was looking for a way of learning to be with God more fully through learning how to read and study scripture in-depth, how to be with God, how eminent Christian figures led their lives, and how I might share what I had come to understand with others in whatever context God might place me.

YTU had a fabulous reputation in theological education. So YTU is where I needed to be to learn how to handle these questions. I came wondering what studying theology was like as my stereotype theologian was well up in the clouds with God or at least in a place like the Vatican or some monastery.

What I found in experiencing YTU was that staff

- were very friendly and would bend over backwards to help both academically and personally.
- were highly regarded in their fields – many working at the highest levels nationally and internationally.
- taught in interesting ways (most were so popular that they had their own 'following' or fan club).
- were accessible (email response times were 1-2 days maximum)

The learning environment both inside and outside the classroom was friendly and conversations were challenging yet engaging. Sharing continued outside the YTU environment with lively discussions taken home and continued with friends. Many long-standing friendships were born.

Highlights of my times at YTU were studying Biblical Interpretation with Mary Reaburn. Coming from the world of nutrition and education, this subject was an initiation indeed as approaches, considerations and the like were far from where I had been previously. It was Mary who introduced me to the considerations and techniques required to plumb scripture in greater depth – enabling me to be with God through his Word much more fully since then.

Method in Theology according to Bernard Lonergan was another highlight both for its content and its delivery by Kathleen Williams. The subject explained the interrelationships between theology, culture, religion and the various theological disciplines and provided the answer to the mystery of how theology operates, thus enabling me to see where the author/s were coming from much more clearly. The subject also provided me with an approach to sound research in theology. Kathleen is a well-respected theologian and a wonderful teacher. Another highlight at YTU was studying Trinity with Jan Gray a brilliant lecturer who had the capacity of communicating a difficult topic incisively. I remember leaving her lectures 'on cloud nine' through her presentations using mostly medieval paintings.

Norman Young taught 'Christ, God for the World' focusing on Jesus Christ: what does scripture say? What does Jesus' incarnation, life, death and resurrection actually mean? What does it mean for us today and what might we do about it? These are profound questions indeed. Norman was another fabulous teacher with an ability to make something complex sound so simple. He was famous for bursting into hymns to illustrate/support his points.

I have fond memories of my time in Larry Nemer's class on 'Early and Medieval Church History' – a wonderful privilege indeed. As a result of taking this subject, I can now relate to differences of opinion within and outside the church and have greater understanding of different perspectives and teachings in theology. Given my interest in Christian mystics, I was thrilled to have the opportunity to study four of them in some depth. Dr Larry was in a class of his own as teacher: warm, friendly, had a wealth of knowledge, and very high standards.

> *Eva Dabasy, nutritionist and educator, was Head, Food Science Department at William Angliss Institute for 25 years. Eva holds a Master of Education, La Trobe University.*

During her tenure, she carried out nutrition consultancies e.g., specialised nutrition training for shift workers, recommendations for nutritionally sound boardroom lunches for ICI Australia (now Orica), audit of the nutritional quality of meals delivered to prisoners at five of Victoria's prisons and nutritional analysis of marketing practices for Coles-Myer National Head Office Marketing Department to inform healthier options. Later, as Manager of Teaching and Learning, Eva contributed to and steered education projects at local, national and international levels, the evaluation of education systems in Indonesia, and presented at conferences in India.

Eva graduated with a Master of Arts (Theology) in 2013 and was Student Representative – Academic Board of the what is now the University of Divinity.[1] Since graduation, Eva has led spirituality days on compassion and gratitude for the Lutheran Women of Victoria, written Lenten devotions, co-led the local parish prayer group and contributed to the parish church delivery of English conversation classes to migrants as a way of mission. Eva has also written a subject on Communicating Theology as part of a Diploma of Theology to be delivered in Papua New Guinea. Eva has contributed to the wider church community through membership of the Advisory Board, Heart of Life, Secretary, Church Council Nunawading-Waverley Lutheran Church and Member, Mission and Ministry Committee. Eva is a member of the Melbourne Lonergan Circle which meets to read and discuss the writings of Bernard Lonergan and practises Christian Meditation.

---

[1] The Melbourne College of Divinity became MCD University of Divinity, and finally the University of Divinity in 2012.

Whoever Would Have Thought: A *Liturgy* Study Tour?

MARGARET SMITH SGS

Whoever would have thought – a **LITURGY** Study Tour? And not just one, but three (2011-13-15)! The thought came from a liturgy student recently returned from a Bible Study Tour that brought the Scriptures alive for him. But LITURGY? Wasn't that, as someone else once said, just about 'pickin' a few 'imms'? Why a study tour when all you needed was a handy hymn book? Simply because liturgy is the heartbeat of the church's life.

The seed having been sown, the idea was explored in 2009 with my liturgical colleagues Deirdre Browne IBVM, Robert Gribben (Uniting Church), Tom Knowles, Frank O'Loughlin and Paul Taylor. We consulted YTU and CTC faculty members who had led biblical, spirituality and catholic culture tours. Their advice was invaluable and their encouragement enthusiastic.

It was the right time. The approach of the 50th anniversary of *Sacrosanctum Concilium* (1963) was generating an abundance of writing about the Liturgical Movement and the implementation of Vatican II's vision of liturgical reform. Serendipitously, the XXII Congress of Societas Liturgica brought international scholars to Sydney in August 2009, providing a unique opportunity for consultation with key liturgical figures who suggested an abundance of people, places and institutes for tour consideration.

The name of the Study Tour – 'Realising the vision: 150 years of liturgical renewal' – was inspired by Archbishop Piero Marini's 2007 book, *Realising the Vision of the Liturgical Renewal 1963-1975*, (eds. Mark Francis, John Page and Keith Pecklers, Collegeville, MN: Liturgical Press, 2007).

The month-long tour, using bases in Cologne, Leuven, Paris, Rome and Trier in order to focus on European centres of the Liturgical Movement and post-conciliar implementation, was approved as a YTU/MCD academic unit in October 2009. It could not have been realised without the belief and strong support of Peter Price and Larry Nemer. The tour included monastic centres such as Maria Laach in Germany where the first dialogue Mass was celebrated in a small crypt in 1921, and three Belgian abbeys – Mont César known especially for its liturgical pioneer, Dom Lambert Beauduin, whose grave we stood beside at the bi-ritual abbey of Chevetogne, and the Monastery of Saint-André de Clerlande, where we met rheumy-eyed Dom Frederic Debuyst, founder and editor of the journal *Art d'Église* for 53 years. Tour participants were privileged to pray with the Jerusalem Communities in Cologne, Paris and Vézelay and the ecumenical monastic communities of Taizé in France and Bose in northwest Italy where the tour concluded with a memorable few days for prayer, reflection and review in an atmosphere of beauty, peace and tranquillity.

The tour was punctuated by presentations from experts in liturgical renewal, research and education, such as Professor Joris Geldhof in Leuven, Professor Patrick Prétot OSB in Paris, and Archbishop Piero Marini, Professors Keith Pecklers SJ and Mark Francis CSV in Rome. Academic liturgical programs were introduced by Professor Albert Gerhards (the University of Bonn) and Professor Ephrem Carr OSB (Pontifical Liturgical Institute, Sant'Anselmo, in Rome). In Rome, dialogue at the Pontifical Council for Promoting Christian Unity was inspirational.

The experience of liturgy in a variety of settings, along with its pastoral outreach, was a key tour ingredient. Sites included St Theodor's with its strong social outreach and a restored Romanesque church St Maria Lyskirchen in Cologne, St-Ignace in Paris (the home base of composer, Joseph Gelineau SJ), the Roman churches of Saint Francis Xavier del Caravita and Santa Maria in Trastevere (used by the Sant'Egidio community for Evening Prayer) and Sant'Ambrogio in Milan. Sunday Evensong at the Anglican Centre in Rome and an Anglican Eucharist at the Caravita Church were memorable highlights.

Church buildings, ancient and new, took their place on the itinerary. Imagine being invited to lie on the sanctuary floor of Cologne cathedral on a wintry night as the darkness deepened, and in this ghostly atmosphere viewing the soaring cruciform ceiling of this vast gothic structure. Paris, by contrast, featured several striking contemporary churches, quite modest in size, located in the heart of business districts, all built for celebration of post-conciliar liturgy.

Cultural experiences extended to a tour of Da Vinci's Last Supper in Milan, organ recitals at Notre Dame and a concert at Sainte Chapelle. The 2011 tour group travelled to Ypres in Flanders on Remembrance Day, 11 November 2021, a day marked by ritual and bone-chilling cold.

Realising the Vision was a unique Australian initiative, and YTU ran with. It was an opportunity for 65 participants over three tours, under the leadership of Margaret Smith SGS, Deirdre Browne IBVM Paul Taylor, Margaret Malone SGS and Stephen Hackett MSC, to be inspired by the work of liturgical renewal from the nineteenth century through to the present day and beyond. Informative speakers, diverse liturgical celebrations and encounters with worshipping communities, exposure to the links between liturgy and social justice, and the experience of the shaping power of liturgical architecture, leavened by travelling companionship and imaginative coach music compiled by Deirdre Browne, all conspired to make the tours a lively and hope-filled experience. Realising the vision? We can't go back, was the message throughout. Amen to that!

> *Margaret Smith (D. Min.) is a Sister of the Good Samaritan. Over the past twenty years, she taught units in liturgical studies in graduate and undergraduate programs at Yarra Theological Union, Catholic Theological College and Broken Bay Institute. Over the years, she served on both Diocesan and National Liturgical Commissions.*

> For several years, Margaret was also on the staff of the then Melbourne Diocesan Liturgical Centre. She has written on the Sacrament of Anointing and the Order of Christian Funerals and writes the annual Children's Daily Prayer Under the Southern Cross. She has conducted numerous workshops on the Church's rites and, in particular, those associated with sickness and death.

YTU, Home to English as a Second Language for Pastoral Ministry

MARGARET BENTLEY FMA

In 1974, as a young candidate with the Salesian Sisters, I began my studies at YTU. I started with one subject – Media Studies with Peter Malone if memory serves me correctly. In 1975, this was extended to two subjects and then my studies were interrupted to begin my Novitiate in the United States. During our media studies, we would gather at one Congregation house or another on a Friday night to watch a movie and have supper together. It was the highlight of our week. What a wonderful way to build networks and support each other in the early days of our vocations. Peter always had a serious message for us about what we should be noticing about the movie, or the hidden meanings inferred in signs and symbols. When I returned to Melbourne a couple of years later, I took up my studies at CTC and greatly missed the comradery and fun that studying at YTU brought with it.

YTU, Home to English as a Second Language for Pastoral Ministry

In 2016, I returned to YTU to take up the position of Academic Manager at the English Language Studies Centre for Pastoral Ministry (ELSPM). To my amazement and great joy, I found the same atmosphere of friendship and support among the religious congregations. I also found a couple of classmates from earlier days and even a buddy from secondary school. It seems that as a Year 12 student at St Columba's in Essendon, my year 7 buddy was none other than Claire Renkin. Luckily, she remembered my group of friends being kind to her and her friends. The Language Centre arrived in July 2015 to take up residence in YTU classrooms during the day. There were 6 students and 4 teachers. It quickly expanded as various Congregations realised that their students could complete their English studies and then move onto YTU with many of the same class companions. The Passionists began the Centre in Adelaide to help their overseas students to obtain a visa to study; they were joined by a group of Dominicans and a couple of priests from the Melbourne Archdiocese. It soon became clear that most prospective students would be in Melbourne and thanks to Fr Chris Monaghan, President of YTU, the Language Centre was able to relocate to YTU. Chris also supported ELSPM in obtaining recognition from the University of Divinity for the English for Academic Purposes program. This enabled students to progress to their Theological studies without sitting outside tests to prove their level of English.

ELSPM past students now number over 200, coming from 33 Religious congregations, 5 Dioceses and 4 other Christian churches. While most continue their studies at YTU, students have also moved on to CTC, Jesuit College, Lutheran College,

Pilgrim, Stirling, and Whitely. Those who do not go on to further study use their English in ministry to obtain a Worker visa for Australia or work in a mission centre that requires English. Others use their language skills to work in their international congregations.

Working again with the Staff at YTU is a privilege; their professionalism, support and understanding, pastoral care and genuine love of the students mark an institution that I am so pleased to be connected with. There is a real understanding that students continue to struggle with English as a second, third or fourth language and that language continues to grow and improve as one experiences life in a new environment. One of the joys of working again in the YTU setting is that past students often pop into the English classrooms and share their progress, or news. Sharing the common room, weekly Masses and other events gives the ELSPM students a broader network, as well as the inspiration to keep at the difficult task of learning English.

> *Margaret Bentley FMA began as the new Academic Manager of ELSPM in September 2016. Margaret is a Salesian Sister and has a life time of work with young people in schools and preschools. She has been Principal of Catholic Primary Schools in New South Wales and Victoria. As Provincial of the Salesian Sisters South Pacific Province for six years, she also built a strong cultural awareness as she worked with the Sisters in Samoa, American Samoa and the Solomon Islands. Margaret brings a wealth of managerial skills to the position as well as her curriculum knowledge and great passion for education.*

Seeking God at Yarra Theological Union – And Through Covid

CARMEL POSA SGS

I have only been privileged to teach in the Department of Christian Thought and History at Yarra Theology Union for just over four years. Two of these years, 2020 and 2021, have been years of the unsettling experience of a global COVID pandemic with all the uncertainty, anxiety, adjustment, and weariness that it brought with it. Yet, I think it is this experience of, what Benedict would call, 'the heavy or impossible tasks' of life (cf. RB, *The Rule of St Benedict*, 68), that has ultimately strengthened my initial understanding of YTU's ethos, particularly in terms of its obedience to its formative, pastoral, and theological mission to students and to Church over the past 50 years.

In the Benedictine Rule, one of the primary indications that a new monk belongs to the community is their desire to 'truly seek God' (RB 58:7). As a Good Samaritan Sister of the

Order of St Benedict, one of the first things that impressed me about Yarra Theological Union was the assumption that this quest for God was a central motivating force for both faculty and students inside and beyond the classroom.

Having taught in other theological institutions both here in Australia and in the United States, I had sometimes found myself struggling with how ideals set forth in a theological faculty's stated mission, its curriculum, and its classroom activities – that is, its seeking of God – contrasted with how its managerial systems and functioning within an institutional setting were realised. All the temptations towards hierarchical structuring and elitism, as well as the economic, political, and academic demands that such an institution implies, seemed, all too often, to override and overwhelm the enshrined ideals. Indeed, it has been easy to let cynicism creep into one's thinking in such environments.

It was not until I found myself inserted into the life at YTU that I actually experienced an atmosphere where vision matched practice in any meaningful sense. The principles of Gospel leadership, inclusive community, pastoral concern and community engagement form the driving force integral to the educational and formative edifice of the College. At first, I found this rather disconcerting. To find yourself sincerely welcomed, your voice sincerely encouraged, and given a safe space for expression, your concerns acted upon with an air of support, and your own unique slant on the issues of theological education appreciated, both through rigorous critique and respectful dialogue, was – well – liberating to tell the truth.

When the pandemic interrupted all so-called 'normal' operations with the cessation of 'face-to-face' learning and meeting schedules, one would have expected some of these ideals to be overridden by practical necessities and the sheer weight of the massive shifts required to keep the College operational. However, it was not through authoritative and disembodied missives about what we must do to continue our teaching mission to students that issued forth from 'above' so that the institution might survive. Rather, it was through a calm concern for all – staff as well as students – that the necessary adjustments were discussed, enabling 'the confident to continue to have something to strive for, and the anxious had nothing to run from' (cf. RB 64:16). It was through this thoroughly incarnational spirit of collaborative consultation that we found ourselves, in spite of it all, still 'One Body', all working together to find a viable path forward with the resources we had and those we could harness to our aid. As Benedict asserts, all things were arranged so that were was no disquiet in the house of God (cf. RB 31:19). Every voice, even that of the newest member of faculty or student body, mattered in this crisis, every idea appreciated and listened to in a continual concern for the community's coherence (cf RB 3). What I found impressive in all this was that the priority of 'seeking God' in the midst of crisis was not sacrificed for more pragmatic ends.

COVID could well have led to a breakdown in the YTU community, but instead it led to a more cohesive sense of mission and outreach. It came to be seen as an opportunity for innovation rather than demise, and this certainly stretched our sense of the Gospel imperatives. We remained a Eucharistic community in the true sense of the word, even though we could not gather. Even though we were unable to share the same space, Christ was incarnated among us.

YTU is, and I'm sure always has been, a place of 'seeking God', where all, staff and students, experience something of the possibility of the Gospel in our broken world. It is a space where we explore the meaning of 'preferring Christ above all else' as we journey all together to everlasting life (cf. RB 72: 11-12).

> Sister Carmel Posa is a member of the Good Samaritan Sisters. She completed her doctoral studies through the Melbourne College of Divinity which was at that time an affiliate of Melbourne University. The title of her thesis was: 'Neither more than a Christian nor more than a woman - Nec plusquam christianae appeteremus esse: The Theology and Spirituality of the Body in the writings of Heloise of the Paraclete'. Carmel held the position of senior lecturer at Notre Dame University, Australia, from 1999-2012 and was the Executive Director of the New Norcia Institute for Benedictine Studies, at New Norcia, WA from 2012-2017. She joined the staff at Yarra Theology Union in 2018 and is teaching in the Department of Christian Thought and History. She also teaches units at St John's School of Theology at Collegeville, Minnesota, in the area of Monastic Studies.

From Student to Chaplain

Pia Pagotto

It was just after my third and last child was at school that I was looking to get back into the workforce as a teacher but I needed to update somewhat and I was interested in RE so I thought I would give YTU a go which was fortunately close to my home at the time. I didn't know what to expect and I was nervous about getting back into study. Could I manage? Was my brain up to it? Would I fit in?

Enrolment was straightforward although I was gently persuaded to enrol in a Bachelor degree rather than just a Graduate Diploma. I remember laughing thinking the Bachelor would never happen... all those years! I attended the Orientation Day and a most friendly lady greeted me as I walked into the common room for the very first time with my nerves in a flutter and all my questions weighing heavily. It didn't take long for the friendly lady to introduce herself, Glenda Bourke, one of the lecturers... and what was I enrolled for in the new semester? The Gospel of Mark, of course, and yes, Glenda had good books she could lend me, no worries! I was stunned, very pleasantly so, at the trust she had in me, in her utter graciousness, no nonsense, no fuss, down to earth way she had, especially considering she was one of the lecturers! I didn't even ask about books, she just volunteered them. Right there I felt totally accepted, graciously welcomed and wonderfully at ease that somehow I could do this.

And I did end up completing a Bachelor which took me ten most happy years and it wasn't just Glenda who was amazingly friendly, helpful and welcoming. Every single lecturer, as well as the resident Franciscans and all the staff, was a delight in their own way, their love of their area of interest, their enthusiasm, their deep-down gentleness and understanding, their desire to help and go the extra mile. Even the librarians were so satisfyingly helpful that I felt like hugging them all the time. With great wonder on my part, each topic took me down what felt like a rabbit hole into deeper and deeper mysteries. I had begun with so many questions and emerged with so many more but now feeling infinitely ok with that. Not getting to the bottom of things with solid answers I could hold in my head (which I guess was what I was initially looking for) became a comfortable and even joyful not-knowing in my heart that felt good.

After the Bachelor, I felt drawn to the Siloam program at Heart of Life, at the time located on the same grounds as YTU, and becoming a Spiritual Director. At the end of that time, I saw an advertisement asking for a Chaplain at YTU. My heart leapt when I read it and I began as Chaplain the following year in 2013 for the next four years. My experiences at YTU, as well as of YTU, had been so wonderful that I really wanted other students to experience the same. This time I was staff and I always remembered Glenda especially and that very first impression that imprinted itself in me and I wanted likewise to be a gracious, welcoming, accepting and helpful presence. I made it a strong basis of my time as a Chaplain to exemplify all that I had myself experienced as a student that made my time so special and happy, and to be present to all. Chris Monaghan OP (President) called what I did a ministry of presence... I like to think that was certainly the case.

> *Pia Pagotto currently (and for over 25 years) works for the Presentation Family Project facilitating (mostly) sacramental workshops for families in parishes. She also works as a Spiritual Director and is significantly engaged in various ministries in her parish. Family concerns are considerable with grandparenthood imminent.*

YTU, Studies and Chaplaincy

Susan Richardson PBVM

Yarra Theological Union first came to my attention in 1982 when I was appointed Formation Director of the Presentation Sisters Central Noviciate in Melbourne. At that time, various programs were offered to students in formation. With the novices, we studied Faith and the Human Life Cycle in Field D, Christology, Spirituality Seminars, Prayer in Christian Spirituality in Field C and Biblical Theology in Field B. If I remember correctly, at that time there were no lay students studying at YTU. All were seminarians, religious sisters and brothers and priests. And, of course, I had very little to do with the faculty other than being at lectures. But one delightful connection was to discover that the YTU accountant at that time, Bernie Barnwell, was a distant relative to the Barnwell Presentation Sisters who established the Lismore Presentation Congregation in 1886. It was a revelation to Bernie, but he recounted the time when his forebears also came out from Ireland to Australia. It wasn't long after that, that Bernie retired.

After many years as a spiritual director, pastoral supervisor and seminar presenter at Heart of Life, in 2012 I completed my Master of Arts (Theology). It was at this time that I got to know the faculty and students, including the many lay students who now attended YTU because of the changes in the Catholic Education System that now employed many lay teachers. The two lecturers that stand out for me were Peter Price and Philip Malone MSC. Both were very encouraging to continue my studies and appreciated my many years of experience as a seminar presenter in the field of Discernment, Psychology and Mysticism, so I could study for my MA without having to complete a BA.

In 2016, Chris Monaghan, the President of YTU approached me about taking on the role of chaplain. This I accepted for a three-year term. My time as chaplain enabled me to be more in touch with the students as well as the faculty. The highlight of the week for me was celebrating Eucharist at lunch time on a Tuesday. This involved inviting the Celebrant from the various male religious congregations – some on faculty – inviting the various students to be readers and helping me to set up the altar in the students' common room. One of the major blessings for the students and some faculty who gathered to celebrate Eucharist on a Tuesday in the student common room was that it gave the student seminarians an opportunity to celebrate in a much more personal and creative way. Apart from the weekly celebration of the Eucharist, I also attended faculty meetings and the student representative council meetings. Every so often, students approached me for some personal help as they dealt with issues they were dealing with in their community, their parish or with one of the other students or faculty.

During my time as chaplain at YTU, I was also the Vicar for Religious for the Melbourne archdiocese. It was a good combination, because I was able to cross pollinate both ministries. Already, there were more religious students from overseas studying at YTU as well as establishing communities in Melbourne. English being their second language meant that I often had to aid them both in English pronunciation as well as cultural issues that needed attention. YTU was also assisted by the English Second Language program established by the Passionists. I was also involved as a pastoral councillor for the ESL program, which made it an opportunistic time to get acquainted with the students who would then go on to study theology at YTU. I certainly am grateful to YTU for all those years of ministry.

> *Sue Richardson is a Lismore Presentation Sister. She has a background in secondary education and has specialised in formation for ministry since 1982. First as formator in the Presentation Sisters Central noviciate program and then as formator for those preparing for final vows. At the same time, Sue was also involved in the formation of spiritual directors in the Siloam and Spiritual Leaders programs, and supervision of pastoral associates, congregation leaders and parish priests at the Heart of Life Centre, where she was twice the Director. Sue has experience in leadership of her congregation for five years.*

> *She also held the office of vice-president of Catholic Religious Australia for three years and for five years was a member of the Council for Clergy Life and Ministry, a council of the Australian Catholic Bishops Commission for Church Ministry. She is currently working in the Emerging Futures program for local congregations.*

YTU – A Lighthouse

GARY HARKIN

My overwhelming impression of my years at YTU is an aura of equality, care and respect to all and among all. In short, it is an inviting and wonderful place. From first contact, the atmosphere is familial, warm and inclusive. There is a lack of the trappings of authority and power. In the best tradition of Australian culture, everyone is on a first name basis. Faculty and Administration staff alike have always been approachable and encouraging. In Gilbert and Sullivan's *The Gondoliers*, Don Alhambra gleefully sings, 'When everyone is somebody then no one's anybody'. Certainly not at YTU.

This outstanding quality of YTU is an exceedingly significant reality. Why? Clearly, there is much of the oxymoron here. Really? A Church-related organisation characterised by equality and respect? If the YTU community is a microcosm of the greater Church and I believe it is, then its culture and mores are very different. We have all been busy in our prayers towards the success of the Fifth Plenary Council of Australia, striving to listen to the Spirit. It often seems to me that the Holy Spirit is active already, perhaps present in November 2012 when Prime Minister Julia Gillard announced the decision to establish the Royal Commission into Institutional Responses to Child Sexual Abuse, surely an important forerunner of change in our Church.

Vincent Long (Bishop of Parramatta), speaking to a group of Vincentians, has spoken thus:

> ... the hierarchical and patristic structures of the Church had led to a lack of kindness and charity, to a travesty of the gospel, and to the virus of misogynism.
>
> 2/5/2018 to the St Vincent de Paul Society (Victoria), 2018 Ozanam Conversation.

Surely this 'virus of misogynism' is at the heart of the catastrophe that is the Church in the 21st. century. The clearly documented absence of appropriate governance regarding the care of children in the Church over many years points to the absolute necessity of women at the top table, where the authority presides.

What is the link to YTU? Clearly at YTU there is no holding back women. YTU is a lighthouse within the Church, a shining light.

Are we getting anywhere? I think so. In 2016, I accepted my B.Theol award at St Paul's Cathedral. My Irish ancestors who unselfishly committed their pennies to our magnificent St Patrick's Cathedral might have looked askance but to me it was a sign of change.

To YTU – many happy returns.

> *Gary Harkin is a parishioner of St Thomas the Apostle, Blackburn, a nearby parish to YTU where there is a good tradition of laity enrolment at YTU.*

Relishing a Golden Opportunity

DANIEL MAGADIA MSC

Coming out of a fruitful and memorable year as a novice, during the 'coronovitiate', it was off to a new chapter, now as a professed MSC. It meant a return to a familiar place, but within a new context. First, I have grown so much since I first entered the congregation back in 2019. Also, there were some new housemates, and a new formator in Mark Hanns MSC. Of course, there was the 'new normal' of the post-COVID world. Despite this, the MSC formation house in Blackburn (also known as Cuskelly House) is still paradise, to quote another well-respected formator, Frank Dineen MSC.

The bulk of the period after novitiate is theological studies. Prior to joining the MSCs, I had already completed a Bachelor's degree in theology. So, part of me was excited to return to academic life. I had heard great things about YTU from confreres who had been either students or lecturers there.

This reinforced said excitement. The counteracting feeling was trepidation, because of the many assessments that would stand on the path of completion.

Upon entering the quaint, but hallowed, grounds of Yarra Theological Union for the first time, I was quickly captured by its tranquillity. It felt like entering a monastery or a friary. Considering the college's Franciscan heritage, it was to no surprise that the courtyard had a sculpture of St Francis of Assisi. It was while marvelling at the simplicity and beauty of the place that I was introduced to YTU's mascots, the adorable guinea pigs. It is an environment conducive for learning and even contemplation.

Cute rodents and serenity aside, a quality worth highlighting has been the school's strong sense of community, making YTU a very welcoming and accepting place. There is a warmth radiating from the lecturers and students. Another notable feature is its diversity. I have had classmates from every corner of the world, from Mexico, Sri Lanka, Thailand, Vietnam, and Timor Leste, just to name a few. A variety of religious congregations were present too, from the Carmelites to the Redemptorists, the Passionists to the Divine Word Missionaries. I even had classmates from other denominations and faiths.

The subjects themselves covered different fields of Theology. I found the classes fun and engaging, and I have learned so much. In scripture, I have had units on Romans and my favourite Gospel, Luke. These were taught by current YTU president, scripture scholar and avid cyclist Chris Monaghan cp. It was also a privilege to be under the tutelage of Robyn Reynolds OLSH, where we tackled Catholic Social Teaching, especially from an indigenous perspective. I realise that Robyn has contributed in every stage of my formation journey so far, from presenting the history of the OLSH sisters, to encouraging me to express myself artistically.

Having a confrere as a lecturer was an interesting, at times hilarious dynamic. Philip Malone MSC, who happens to also be the community superior, was my moral theology professor. My most valuable insight from him was the importance of 'why' in moral Christian living. He also taught me liturgy, where I developed a greater appreciation of the insights of *Sacrosanctum Concilium*. Staying on liturgy, sessions with Gavin Brown was always enlightening. His unit on Sacrament Theology was one of my favourites. Theologian Louis-Marie Chauvet's fanbase has grown, thanks to Gavin's class.

Looking back at my first year at YTU as a whole, it was the tale of two semesters. I considered myself lucky that the first semester of 2021 was not affected too much by COVID-19, with all sessions face-to-face. Semester two was something else. This was the first time I experienced university done entirely online, especially over the program Zoom, which had its unique set of challenges. I must confess, studying at Master's level was intimidating, especially with writing big essays and enduring long lockdowns. It tested my energy, and my ability to stay organised, flexible, and motivated. The moments of insights, stress, and even procrastination, were opportunities for growth.

As for highlights, there were many. Aside from the learning, one worth mentioning was getting to Box Hill for morning classes. If weather permitted, I often walked through the parklands, either silently or while listening to music or a podcast. This would also satisfy my exercise quota that day. Another was witnessing the final professions and ordinations of schoolmates. Cheering my classmates on during the annual soccer tournament, the Brotherhood Cup, has been a highlight too. Even the conversations, laughter and banter amongst seminarians in the common room were moments I would treasure. Of course, there were the feelings of triumph and relief whenever I would finish and submit a long paper.

As I embark on my second year of studies at YTU, what are my hopes for 2022? The obvious ones are to learn more, and, of course, in the end to pass. I have only four units to go in my Master's course. The ones I have enrolled in this year are taking me to uncharted waters. This is especially true for my two units on Canon Law, being taught by Rosie Joyce CSB. To my surprise, it is a subject I am enjoying so far. I admire how she makes the code understandable and practical, and how she reminds us of the primary purpose of the law: the salvation of others, not to burden them. Returning to the title, I also hope to continue to maintain this sense of fun and enthusiasm. As for future, I hope YTU continues to shape more people, especially MSC's, to be sound and pastoral theologians in the decades to come.

I thank God and his divine providence, and also the Missionaries of the Sacred Heart, for the golden opportunity to study at YTU.

> Daniel Magadia is currently a professed student for the Australian province of the Missionaries of the Sacred Heart. Born in the Philippines, his family moved to South Australia during his teenage years, and it was there that he met the MSCs. Before joining, he worked in hospitality and was active in youth ministry, while studying for his Bachelor's course in Theology.

Thank you, from Janette Bredenoord Elliott, Registrar 2009-2022

JANETTE ELLIOTT

God – First and foremost, I thank God for leading me – with my future husband at the time – to this place – YTU on this beautiful Franciscan property - of welcome, inclusivity and acceptance. These are priceless treasures that I will always hold dear.

Original Owners of the Land – I would like to acknowledge with respect the indigenous people of this land, the Kulin nations, and in particular the Wurundjeri people of Melbourne.

Franciscan Friars and to my husband – I would like to express my deep, deep gratitude to the Franciscan Friars for their generosity over the past 50 years to YTU from its earliest beginnings, and making possible the formation of hearts and minds in such a glorious setting. I remember with fondness the Guardians, Steve Bliss and Jordie Warburton, and all the Friars who made this place and YTU such a rich centre of prayer and learning.

In my role as Registrar (and maybe personally too), I want to thank Noel Elliott - Honorary Friar - for his skilled art in keeping these grounds of St Paschal Estate so beautiful. Noel encapsulates everything about stewardship of care, respect and love for this place and the grounds that is quintessentially Franciscan. For the deep joy this has brought to me and to so many others - Thank you, Mr Elliott!!

Students Past and Present - To the students - how lucky am I to have had you at my farewell. The attraction of this position when I started was for others that is YOU to experience the wonder of studying theology so as to know the length and the breadth, the height and the depth of knowing God's love for all people. You give SONG to YTU and represent the best that society and culture offer - accepting difference and diversity - most especially, multi-cultural diversity. Thank you for the joy and hope you give us all.

Faculty - to the Dear Faculty, Past and Present, and those who have gone before especially Larry Nemer, Peter Price, Glenda Bourke, and Angelo O'Hagan among others. I have learned so much from your passion for what you do, how you go about your teaching and research - both in every and the fullest sense. You all give so generously to YTU, to students and your encouragement of me in my own academic endeavours. Thank you -each of you - from my heart.

YTU Council - To the Provincials past and present and other members of Council. It have been a real privilege to be among

Thank you, from Janette Bredenoord Elliott, Registrar 2009-2022

you who are passionate, unassuming, humble and utterly faithful to the Gospel of Jesus Christ. You embody what we desire church to be and become. In sending students to YTU, in serving on committees and sharing expertise and resources, your embodiment is made flesh and YTU would not continue without your support in all these ways.

YTU Extended Family - Alumni, Staff, Faculty and Friends of YTU - you carry the torch of faith, passion and compassion in loving service in your life. I would like to thank in a special way the Community of Dorish Maru. Kasmir, Bosco and Anton were the first friends we made here at the Blessing of the Study Centre. The hospitality shared at Dorish Maru through Larry Nemer was of another realm! Here I also want to pay tribute to the generous resources made available via YTU's constituent orders. This extends from I.T. resources through Michael Mason CSsR to the gift of presence of Heart of Life through Brian Gallagher MSC, and those who followed: Sue Richardson and Paul Beirne. Thank you.

UD Staff, Registrars and Admin Assistants - To Peter and to University Staff, Past and present especially John, Rose, Tricia, Anna and Arezoo - with the extended network of College Registrars and their colleagues, I am grateful for all that I have learned from you and our shared support system.

St Paschal Library and Associated Libraries - I would like to acknowledge all the Librarian staff that I have worked with during my time going back to Thea, Miranda, Leonie and Siobhan to the new team of Nick, Sai and Ben. Your love for your work and your generous service of students and Faculty witnesses to the richness of all that takes place on the St Paschal Estate.

Chaplain – to Steve, Pia, Sue, Rachel and to Jill. Your presence makes more difference than you may possibly know. The place you hold is precious and, while seemingly small, weaves the Spirit through the day-to-day running of YTU.

Admin – When I began at YTU, there were no Admin staff and my email was not registrar, but admin specific. The Staff that I have worked with during my time – Carey, Julie, Bernie, Jean, Katrina, Hayley, Nic, Tricia, Katherine and Rose –have all taught me so much. You have taught me so much about professionalism, about learning to listen, about learning to delegate, about so much of workplace operations. I also want to acknowledge the contribution of Margaret Bentley from the English Language School which with those of Admin has been a great blessing. Working also alongside Leonie, Cecilia and Susanah from Heart of Life has added to the quality of the broader 'admin expertise'. Our shared and individual relationships have shaped much of who I have become as Registrar in the unwieldly network of relationships that make up YTU. Thank you from my heart.

Michael Kelly – Thank you for your encouragement and support, professionalism in service in all the capacities I have worked with you in: PG Coordinator, Research Coordinator (and 'my' Research Coordinator up until recently) whatever the forum. You always have time for people – a quality that I am still learning and working on – while managing a heavy work load.

Ross Fishburn – We hear that YTU is described as 'Catholic in tradition and ecumenical in spirit'. Ross:, you have brought this gallant catch-phrase of YTU' Spirit of ecumenism and inclusivity' alive. Your lived paschal ecclesiology finds profound expression in your service of YTU. Paired with your extraordinary institutional memory brings a quality and depth to your role of Academic Dean that cannot be expressed in words. You truly embody what you teach, and you have taught me much about the value of striving for greater depth in the quality of my learning even day-to-day tasks.

Chris Monaghan – As President of YTU, you embody a leadership style that is in every way and at every level GOSPEL centred – even your stewardship of YTU's resources. Everyone is invited to the table; everyone is welcome, and everyone – however wounded – has a place. You – like Jesus – and as St Paul strived for – encourage us all the 'be the more' of who we can become. You leave us free to respond to the Lord, even with our thorns or 'thorniness'. In this you embody what YTU exemplifies – the place of welcome and of invitation to the more the Lord has to offer.

Ode to YTU

YTU, YTU
You are like Christ, the Mother hen
who gathers the chicks under her wings -
Feeding, nourishing, nurturing – providing a place of welcome, of safety, of refuge, until we grow strong and grow wings to fly,
Wings to soar with faith, hope, courage, compassion and love – taking with us as the 'torch' of YTU for
- speaking the truth in love and being the change we want to see.
TO YTU: BE WHAT YOUR ARE so that we may become who we are called to be as God's Beloved.

Aiming for Excellence

Janette Bredenoord Elliott served as Registrar of YTU from 2010 to 2022. During that time she has also continued doctoral research on Julian of Norwich.

The School of Indigenous Studies at the University of Divinity

The offices of the School are located at the YTU campus.

Wominjeka! Welcome to the School of Indigenous Studies at the University of Divinity.

Launched in 2022, the School's mission is to encourage the development of Aboriginal and Torres Strait Islander theologies and ministries, and to decolonise the eurocentric versions of Christianity that remain dominant in this country.

This will be achieved through:

1. forming respectful relationships with Aboriginal and Torres Strait Islander communities and Elders and with Indigenous councils and assemblies amongst the University's partner churches
2. delivering Aboriginal, Torres Strait Islander, and world Indigenous curriculum in partnership with NAIITS and the University's Colleges
3. encouraging and developing a University-wide research culture that embeds Aboriginal, Torres Strait Islander and world Indigenous methodologies, ontologies, axiology and Indigenous approaches to theology and ministry that seek to inform and challenge the wider church and community.
4. providing a culturally safe and supportive environment for Aboriginal, Torres Strait Islander, and world Indigenous peoples to promote access, retention and success in theology and ministry.
5. continuing to transform the cultures and activities of the University, its Colleges, and partners, to promote justice and equity and to address the impact of colonisation.
6. developing innovative and engaging learning experiences with the wider church and community that foster knowledge, respect and understanding of Aboriginal and Torres Strait Islander histories and knowledge and of shared histories that are purposeful, and transforming.

 **The Reverend Aunty Janet Turpie-Johnstone** is the chair of our School of Indigenous Studies Committee. A woman whose homelands are in Guditjtamara Country, she is a valued board member of two Indigenous controlled organisations in Naarm (Melbourne) and continues to teach about culture at ACU. Aunty Janet is completing a PhD with ANU on Indigenous readings of Naarm landscapes. She is also a retired Anglican priest.

 **The Reverend Dr Garry Deverell** is a Trawloolway man and a Lecturer and Research Fellow within our School. From 2019, Garry chaired the working group that conceived the model for the School and brought it into being. Garry is a theologian of liturgy and sacraments, of Christian community, and of Indigenous experience in the colonised world. He is the author of *Gondwana Theology* (2018) and *The Bonds of Freedom* (2008) as well as multiple journal articles and book chapters.

National Centre for Pastoral research

This is an agency of the Australian Catholic Bishops Conference. The Centre has set up a Melbourne office, in association with the University of Divinity on the YTU Campus.

Postscript

In the 1980s especially, there was the annual revue. Tony Kelly CSsR usually presented a poem of his own creation, incorporating his wide, very wide, vocabulary, with touches of the idiosyncrasy. This one comes from 1983, in the wake of Australia's victory at yachting in the America's Cup. (For best effect, it needs to be heard with Tony's accents and pauses...) Tony is also paying tribute to the first women on the YTU staff: Kath Moynihan, registrar, Loretto Sister Joan Nowotny, Academic Dean, Sister of Charity, Marianne Confoy, Bridgidine Sister, Margaret Jenkins, and counselling course lecturer, Mary Scarfe.

The YTU Yacht: Revue 1983

It may be that some do choose
To see YTU as a Yarra cruise.
As they read on the deck or contemplarively snooze.
But to the toiling crew as they keep it up

YTU is a yacht in the America's Cup:
A syndicate of Provincials watches from the shore,
Commending each victory and shouting 'Encore!';
A flotilla of Formators scans us with powerful glasses,
Asking insistently, Why don't they move their muscles?
Still, the crew toils on, nothing ignored,
Despite the odd storm and the students overboard (bored?):
For us, the race! The Gold and the Green
Takes to the water like a great submarine:
Come MCD missile or Senate torpedo,
We stay down under and remain incognito;
If it's Vatican depth charge we have reason to fear,
Well, we breeze along and stay up here.

But, oh, the YTU yacht's perfection of line –
Many B.Theol. points in her design:
Her philosophical hull of solid Dutch plan,
Her historical ballast and sales of spiritual span,
Her moral balance, her pastoral trim,
Liturgically light, and in the missiological swim,
The best R.E. Rigging and a big biblical anchor:
She's as safe and as precious as any great tanker;
She tacks and she jibes, you ecstatically feel,
Because of that special extra, the Systematic-ally winged keel.

If you would water-ski across the waves,
You have a whole faculty of rowing galley slaves.

So our yacht through wild waters does lurch
Magnificently manned by 'our women in the Church'.
There she is, mistress of boom and Jib,

Postscript

She, for the sake of the rhyme, is James Joseph's rib.
She, always the oil on the troubled water,
The outgoing SRC secretary, Anita Fergus-daughter.
But there are on the prow, just back from Wales,
Creating storm and commanding the gales,
Stands our Dean with green handbook (finally) displayed,
Sternly, Triumphantly – she who must be obeyed!
All hands are silent when on 'Dean's Business' she speaks;
For, as I say, just back from Wales she knows about the leaks* (a cultured pun).
And then, down below, in cabin watertight,
All-knowing, all-seeing, yet hidden from sight,
His midship-person, Kath, from Erin's green Isle,
Watching the compass and checking each style,
Possessor of patience, an inexhaustible quota:
When the breezes don't blow, and the rowers don't row,
She just starts the motor.

By her side, an oyster pearling in its shell,
Typing away is petty-officer Pratt, Estelle.
There, high in the foc'sle, defying the wind,
Another Abelseaperson, now dramatically thinned,
The toast of the convoy, Maryanne Confoy:
By paddling her life-cycle through faith to hope,
She energetically assists the whole crew to cope.
Then, on a non-, evermore impelled to thanks,
We could work through all the other ranks:
E.g., That artful marine, sacramental Brigidine,
Sister Margaret Jenks.*(SLIGHT MISPRONUNCIATION NECESSARY).
And, should the cause waver or the sails droop,
Mary Scarfe is ready to counsel any dispirited group.

All in all, though their patience is sore tried,
The YTU crew battles the tide:
The Captain, of course, always along for the ride,
Is well occupied fishing over the side.

So, now, all hands on deck to drink and to sup
In celebrating our victory in the America's Cup:
Here we are, from fore and aft,
Convivially sharing a generous draft!
Our toast, not to winning – that is oft remote,
But to the magical, splendid fact that we float
In this mysterious, improbable, wonderful boat.

Looking Forward to What Comes Next in our Life

CHRISTOPHER MONAGHAN CP,
President of YTU

> The joys and the hopes, the griefs and the anxieties of the men of this age, especially those who are poor or in any way afflicted, these are the joys and hopes, the griefs and anxieties of the followers of Christ. Indeed, nothing genuinely human fails to raise an echo in their hearts.
>
> *Gaudium et Spes,*

The opening words of *Gaudium et Spes* are as fresh and relevant today as they were in 1965 and they have had an enormous impact on the vision and mission of YTU. When

I began my ministerial studies in 1974, just two years after YTU was accredited to teach seminarians, the church was humming, and so was YTU. How were future generations going to be prepared for ministry? How did the church understand its presence and its function in the modern world? The dynamic nature of the scriptures as both human and divine was reaffirmed, and it had been clearly stated that truth comes to us in a variety of ways. This opened pathways for all sorts of questions to be explored with freedom and enthusiasm.

As a pilgrim people, it didn't take long for our founding congregations and orders to realise that preparing seminarians for ordination was best done in an environment where they were rubbing shoulders with other religious, both men and women, and with the people of God they would serve. Rough edges were rubbed off, uninformed presuppositions challenged and a vibrant and diverse learning community was created. There was a strong sense of being prepared and challenged so that we could serve and adapt to whatever was going to be needed. We were all on this journey together and this is a journey that has continued unabated with the passing of the years. If anything, the sense of mission and the conviction that we do this together, has only strengthened over the decades.

As we celebrate these fifty years by looking at our past, and contemplating our mission in the future, it seems most opportune that it coincides with the Plenary Council and Pope Francis' call for a synodal church. YTU is a community of communities and each of the charisms of our religious institutes reminds us of the many and varied ways in which the Holy Spirit has worked through our founding charisms. Our religious faculty members are a living snapshot of consecrated life in its various expressions over the centuries. Each charism brings some richness to the life of YTU as these charisms continue to resound in many new settings and cultures. Dialogue, careful listening, and leadership that is for a time and then relinquished are hard-wired into our communal structures and have much to offer the church at this time.

The moral and financial support of so many religious orders, congregations and societies has provided us with the resources and confidence to rise to many challenges over the last fifty years. Without the generosity and extraordinary support of the Friars Minor, YTU would not have had a home, a study centre, or a place to house our library collection. It is impossible to overestimate their commitment to our College that continues to this day. So many faculty members have come from our constituent orders and their commitment to the life of YTU has been considerable. There is not sufficient space to mention them all here but suffice to say that as you look through the many reflections in this volume you'll hear their names: Tony Kelly CSsR, Jerome Crowe CP, Angelo O'Hagan OFM, Campion Murray OFM, Kees de Kuyer CSsR, Peter Malone MSC, Larry Nemer SVD to name but a few. We are very grateful for that ongoing commitment to theological education when they have had many other legitimate calls on their resources for other aspects of the church's mission.

So many of our faculty have been selected and trained by our religious institutes with a view to making them available to teach at YTU, and I am but one example. It has not just been about the men and I want to highlight the contribution of many women's orders. It has been considerable and I want to honour that by mentioning a few: Margaret Jenkins, Rosie Joyce (CSB), Maryanne Confoy (RSC), Diedre Browne, Joan Nowotny and Rachel McLoughlin (IBVM), Kathleen Williams, Jan Gray, and Elizabeth Dowling (RSM), Carmel Posa, Catherine McCahill, Glenda Bourke, Marg Smith, Jill O'Brien (SGS), Mary Coloe (PBVM), Mary Reaburn (NDS), and Robyn Reynolds (OLSH). We have much to be grateful for because each of these extraordinary women has contributed their gifts of wisdom and their passion for the message of Jesus and the mission of the church in the world.

Another charism that is vital to the life of YTU is that shared by our lay faculty who embody the commitment to learning, service, justice; and a model of Church where everyone contributes their gifts to build up the body of Christ. Their commitment to YTU is demonstrated by their passionate engagement, teaching and research. We are deeply indebted to their preparedness to teach and research for remuneration that is not nearly as much as they deserve, or representative of how highly they are esteemed as educators and colleagues. At a time when the Church is consistently challenged to address clericalism in life-giving ways, the gift of having so many dedicated lay faculty is impossible to overestimate. We are so blessed to have the contributions of lay faculty from the beginning such as Mary Scarfe, Claire Renkin; Rose Marie Prosser, Gavin Brown, Cecilia Francisco-Tan, John Collins, and Peter Price who was taken from us much too soon.

We pride ourselves on our spirit of welcome and

hospitality and this begins when you walk in the door and head up to reception and are greeted by Nicole Ross and Katherine Blyth who are so willing to assist in whatever way they can. They stand in a long and rich tradition going back Kathleen Moynihan and Estelle Pratt.

We describe our College as Catholic in tradition and ecumenical in spirit. This is nowhere more evident than looking at the simple fact that Ross Fishburn, our Academic Dean for over ten years, is an Anglican Priest. Our new Registrar Adam Couchman describes himself as an Anglo-Catholic Salvationist, and our Associate Dean John McDowell speaks of himself as Catholically Reformed. If this doesn't indicate our commitment to a spirit of dialogue and welcome, I'm not sure what would. How could a college not be enriched by luminaries such as Christiaan Mostert and Norman Young who continued to teach at YTU after their retirement at Uniting Faculty of Theology? Norman brought the wealth of his vast experience as a moderator of the Methodist Church and played a key role in the establishment of the Uniting Church in Australia. His collaboration in lecturing for many years with Aloysius Rego OCD was one of such mutual respect, dialogue and care that it incarnated so many of our hopes and dreams for ecumenism. Both Chris' and Norman's teaching and their contribution to Faculty Research Seminars were always greatly valued, providing opportunities to broaden our vision and understanding of the many issues so close to our hearts.

Vulnerability is something that has always been a part of our experience and while it has its moments, there is always a gift in it. The ability to adapt to changing circumstances and to use the resources available to us creatively is an important feature of YTU's story. We have never had the luxury of feeling complacent because each chapter in the life of YTU brings new challenges and invitations to respond to the signs of the times and the promptings of the Spirit among us.

Not having all the resources and answers is a very Gospel place for us to be. Faculty can be called to leadership or transferred. Financial support can be withdrawn or limited due to other needs of the missions of our congregations and orders. We cannot take things for granted and this invites us to be creative with what we have, determine what is most important, and give of ourselves planting and nurturing what we can. The strength of YTU is always to be found in the relationships that are built on faith, hope and love. The founder of my own religious congregation St Paul of the Cross said that the love of God is ingenious and he had a profound belief in God's loving providence. It has seemed to me over the years that God always finds a way, opens an unexpected door, and reveals a new possibility if we are listening and our mission is attuned to God's loving purpose and the needs of the community.

Looking back over my time as President of the College, there have been many developments and challenges. In 2012, the Melbourne College of Divinity became the first University of specialisation in Australia. It was a big transition for MCD and its Colleges that brought increasing administrative loads for faculty and staff. There were many systems and policies to develop and YTU faculty generously played their part in establishing new committees. In fact, on one occasion I was approached and gently informed that YTU didn't have to volunteer for everything! What this indicates is just how generously our faculty responded to the invitation to contribute their time and energy.

Responding to the challenges that COVID has imposed on us provides a perfect illustration of how new opportunities for outreach and engagement present themselves. Over two weeks, we had to suddenly make the transition to teaching our units online. They say that you can't teach old dogs new tricks but that is far from describing what came to pass. There is no doubt that it involved a great deal of work but the end result is that now units are taught face-to-face and online in real time with students logging in from other countries and time zones. One of the biggest developments has been how this technology has opened opportunities for us to engage with much wider audiences.

Our faculty has always been active in working with and for parishes and teachers. Working in partnership with Garratt Publishing, we offer Lenten and Advent programs, seminars such as *Women Called to Be Dangerous*, *Building the Church We Need*, and *Interfaith dialogue*, to name but a few. Where we might have previously presented a talk to fifty or a hundred people, now YTU sessions may have one thousand registrations. The partnership with Garratt has also produced a number of Friendly Guides in the scriptures from Mary Coloe, Janina Hiebel, Mary Reaburn and myself.

One of the great joys of University graduations is that of seeing our students when they are presented to the Chancellor to receive their testamurs. I often turn to those Principals beside me to comment on a particular student's journey, struggles and achievements. For some, it's academic excellence, for others just getting there at all is a testimony to their dedication, love and commitment. To celebrate their journey and the possibilities that open up for them because of their theological studies is a joy for us as faculty. Many students come to theological studies for professional development and formal ministerial training but there are those who undertake their students because something deep inside prompts them to explore their faith and grow as disciples. Knowing that our graduates are involved in making the world a warmer, kinder and more humane one is something that impels us forward. We have graduates who work as missionaries throughout the world and closer to home as educators, pastors, counsellors, pastoral associates, teachers, religious educators, school principals, and even a few bishops: Paul Bird CSsR, Anthony Fisher OP, Greg Homeming OCD, Vincent Long OFMConv, and most recently, Tim Norton SVD.

There are so many thanks to extend to those who are all precious threads in the tapestry of YTU's life over fifty years. We give thanks for the courage and vision of the founding vision to put out into the deep and try something new. At every level, people have been so overwhelmingly generous in giving their time and energy: YTU Council members, Presidents, Academic Deans, Registrars, Administration staff, Faculty members, Tutors, Chaplains, Peer Contact Officers, Librarians, Business Administrators, Department Heads, Research Coordinators, Academic and Education Board members, Finance and Business Development Committee members, Occupational Health and Safety Committees, Student Representative

Councils, benefactors, friends, and alumni.

It has been a great source of joy for me to have studied, taught, and served as President since 2009. To work closely for over ten years with Ross Fishburn and Janette Bredenoord as our College executive has been a precious gift and I want to thank them in particular for sharing in the journey during these years.

This volume is filled with reflections and memories and there is so much to savour, ponder and reflect on. I'm looking forward to what comes next in the life of our College. We will face it as we always have with love, dedication, good humour, scholarship, passion and listening to the promptings of the Holy Spirit.

> *Chris Monaghan is a Passionist who studied at YTU and then at the Pontifical Biblical Institute in Rome and Jerusalem. Since 1987, he has been lecturing at YTU in both Old and New Testament. The major focus of his teaching throughout these years has been Matthew, Luke-Acts, and the letters of Paul. During this period, Chris has been engaged in adult education programs through schools, parishes, and ministry to priests. Making the Bible in its richness accessible to people at all levels is an enduring passion.*

www.ingramcontent.com/pod-product-compliance
Lightning Source LLC
Chambersburg PA
CBHW012004090526
44590CB00026B/3865